FRENCH DRAWING

OF THE XVI CENTURY

FRENCH DRAWING
OF THE XVI CENTURY

99 REPRODUCTIONS

Text and notes by

Jean Adhémar

Edited by

Ed. Mermod-Lausanne

A Thames and Hudson Book

THE VANGUARD PRESS

NEW YORK

TEXT PRINTED IN GREAT BRITAIN BY JARROLD AND SONS LTD NORWICH 1955

GRAVURE PLATES PRINTED IN SWITZERLAND BY FRÉDÉRIC WAHLI LAUSANNE

LIST OF PLATES

FRENCH DRAWING
OF THE XVI CENTURY

SIXTEENTH-CENTURY French drawing has never received the attention it deserves. Apart from ten or so excellent pages by Pierre Lavallée, research has been fragmentary and this is, we believe, the first complete study of the subject to be published.

In the upheavals of French history and social change many sixteenth-century portraits and decorative ensembles have disappeared. Seventeenth-century paintings have been more fortunate and many have survived to our day; but the prudery of queens, the carelessness of kings and noblemen, the revolutions and fires, and the rebuilding of châteaux on a larger scale all seem to have combined against sixteenth-century painting. It is paradoxical that drawings should still exist and for many reasons they are well worth our study. One most important reason is that they usually represent the artist's original ideas and are rarely copies of a finished painting; as a result their quality is exceptionally fine. Another reason is that drawing became an independent medium in the sixteenth century for the first time, and collectors formed the first collections of drawings; because of newly developing taste and also because it was quicker than painting, artists began to use chalk. Finally, these drawings must also be studied for the development of French art, which was affected at this time by widely differing influences. There were in consequence various artistic movements, and divergent and often opposed aesthetics added to the turmoil created by war. The French style was formed with difficulty, and artists and collectors alike had continually to start afresh and renew their efforts.

The influence of Jean Fouquet (*c.* 1415–*c.* 1480) and some of his contemporaries must not be forgotten but, as Pierre Lavallée pointed out, it is impossible to study sixteenth-century French drawing without understanding the predominant part played by the Italians in the formation of the French School.

Our point of departure is 1515, the year of Marignano and the year in which Francis I persuaded Leonardo da Vinci to come to France. Leonardo left Italy at the end of 1516 and was settled in the Château of Cloux near Amboise in May 1517. He was then sixty years old and too tired to paint. According to his biographers he did nothing "but draw"—and there is at Windsor a collection of drawings from this "French" period, which was necessarily brief as Leonardo died in 1519.

These "French" drawings have their own characteristic technique. They differ profoundly from earlier drawings done with silverpoint or pen as Leonardo used rather a crumbling charcoal. They are as moving as the last drawings of Degas or Daumier, and like their drawings they show that although visual perception had weakened, inspiration and beauty of technique remained as strong as ever. Leonardo made many drawings in France and the collection which was inherited by his pupil Melzi went first to Italy, and finally to Windsor. The subjects are varied: grotesque heads, as beautifully realized as ever (which the biographers tend to underestimate), ideas for building a château, plans for irrigating the Amboise district and for a canal joining the Loire to the Saône, costume designs for two Court festivals and the beautiful study of a draped figure, either man or woman, who points towards something we cannot see (plates 7, 8 and 6).

Unfortunately, Leonardo died and his studio was dispersed; the other Italians summoned by the King did not stay long in France. The leading draughtsman was now Jean Clouet, who came not from Italy but from Flanders, and who had settled in Touraine on his marriage. He created the genre of chalk portraits. There had been portrait drawing in chalk before and Fouquet had even used pastel; King René kept "portraits drawn in lead" in chests and in his closet there was a "drawing in lead" of Francesco Sforza. But Clouet was the first to use chalk as an independent medium and it was owing to his influence that the number of chalk drawings increased so rapidly. Madame Bouchot-Saupique has said that they are "the documents of the period, health bulletins, portraits connected with marriage contracts, and often preparatory sketches for a portrait when the model did not want to be bored by lengthy sittings". Jean Clouet excelled in these preparatory sketches, for which he often used silverpoint—unfortunately they are now rare. He caught the essential likeness with a spirit inherited from Perréal perhaps or the pupils of Raphael. His first drawings done from about 1515 to 1520 are the best, and they are a sort of trial of strength. Later he used a greasier crayon for heavily-shaded portraits which have always been very popular although they have not the same fine quality as his earlier work. He was then living in Paris and was much appreciated at Court for his skill and fidelity to the model. Fillon quotes a letter written to Francis I by the wife of Artus Goufier when she sent him a chalk drawing of the future Henry II by Clouet—"I am giving the messenger a portrait of your little Henry on a sheet of paper so that you can see what he is like now." Moreover, at this very time, in 1524, Holbein travelled across France and from then on according to Ganz he gave up silverpoint for the coloured chalk which Clouet used. Clouet had certainly created a new genre which reached its full development after 1548.

In 1530 Rosso arrived in Paris. The King had been so impressed by one of his drawings that he had summoned him to the Court. The subject—Cupids divesting Mars of his helmet and sword while the Graces attended Venus—had been inspired by Aretino. This allegory alluded to the second marriage of Francis I and his decision not to declare war against the House of Austria.

Sensuous, pleasant, and harmonious, this drawing was a great success in France. The original as far as we know has disappeared but there are numerous pen-and-ink copies in existence. Rosso probably used sanguine as he did for other drawings of the same period, such as *La Vierge de la Miséricorde* (1529–30) originally intended for Arezzo but brought to France instead (plate 17).

The King must have been surprised when he saw the first drawings that Rosso did at Fontainebleau as they are quite different from the drawings of 1529. He had gone to a lot of trouble to persuade Rosso to come to Paris to celebrate his triumphs and in the meantime Rosso's style had become hard and tragic in feeling. He no longer uses sanguine but pen-and-ink and bistre. On the journey through Switzerland, as he travelled from Venice to Paris, he seems to have had some kind of revelation. It must have been at Geneva that he saw paintings by Nicolas Manuel Deutsch from whom he borrowed the motif of trees with hanging foliage. This convention became part of the stock-in-trade of the School of Fontainebleau for more than ten years. From Altdorfer and Cranach Rosso acquired a certain violence and, above all, a nervousness of touch which altered his style beyond recognition.

From now on "awkward, angular, queerly jointed figures with grimacing faces and sharply pointed fingers stream from his cutting pen" (Lavallée). The reason for this transformation, which has always puzzled art historians, lies in Rosso's journey across Switzerland.

Few of his drawings have survived; scarcely three or four for his great work, the *Galerie François I*, which comprised fourteen large panels and many small subjects. The original drawings which were no doubt given to the assistants working under Rosso's supervision must have disappeared with them or in the normal process of painting. The drawings that remain are usually in pen-and-ink heightened with bistre. Their composition is often violent and dramatic with figures twisting in contortions that he had taken over from Bandinelli rather than Michelangelo. He used the bistre wash to give an illusion of depth and modelling so it is not surprising that his drawings had more influence on contemporary sculpture than on painting.

Rosso disappeared in 1540 in mysterious circumstances; very little is known about it apart from Vasari's account which he based on the recollections of Primaticcio, a Bolognese painter and Rosso's rival for the King's favour. Rosso was a violent and moody man and he may have attempted to push Primaticcio aside when the newcomer first began to be successful. This may have been the reason for Primaticcio's journeys to Brussels and Rome. He claimed that Rosso had killed himself after wrongly accusing his friend Pellegrino who had been tortured as a result. This is unlikely because Rosso's body would have suffered the same fate as the body of his compatriot, Bartolomeo di Miniato, a painter with an equally high reputation who killed himself in Paris in 1547. Rosso's body would also have been dragged on a hurdle through the streets and the circumstances would generally have been known. It is much more likely that Rosso could not survive his own jealousy; the King had regarded him as a painter without an equal in 1532, and now he was powerless against a more gifted man.

After Rosso's death in 1540 Primaticcio came to the fore. He had arrived in France in 1532 as a young man of twenty-seven by virtue of his collaboration with Giulio Romano and his imitation of his master's style. Despite an interruption from 1559 to 1563 when the Italians were out of favour, he was a prolific artist right up to his death in 1570. The style of his drawings is invariable. He used pen-and-ink and bistre and above all sanguine heightened with white. His women are exquisitely formed with delicious softness; their grace, elegance and charm make his drawings unforgettable.

"He had great poetic feeling," said Dimier, who praised "the broad and floating shapes of his figures, their contrasting attitudes and the easy graceful carriage of their heads, the charm of his curly-headed, dimpled children, and his use of voluminous draperies which do not enclose the body, but yield and flow from the limbs creating an extraordinary sensation of lightness".

One feels that Primaticcio was not a really great artist: but he had vitality and was full of schemes and ideas. Vasari comments on the "Lombard courtesy" with which he distributed work among his associates; on the other hand, he never hesitated to borrow a good idea from anybody. He was the pupil of Giulio Romano whose frescoes are full of the din of battles (Vatican) or of episodes like the mountains falling on the red giants (Palazzo del Tè, Mantua), and when he arrived in Paris he engaged himself to Rosso whose style was not so very different. Then he discovered Parmigianino. It is most likely that this discovery took place, not at Bologna, but at Fontainebleau when Antonio Fantuzzi arrived there in 1540—Fantuzzi was the new name adopted by Antonio da Trento, a pupil of Parmigianino's. He had stolen his master's drawings and brought them to France in order to turn them to his own advantage. Primaticcio had a great admiration for these drawings. They inspired him and helped him to develop quite a different style from Rosso's and one more in tune with the French temperament. This no doubt accounts for the success of his work which was more overwhelming than any other painter's right up to 1580.

Primaticcio was first and foremost a draughtsman. He painted little himself, and his friend Vasari describes his methods; he would draw the preliminary design and sketch it out on the wall, then his assistants would lay in the colour. Many drawings for the different apartments at Fontainebleau still exist (plates 20, 21, 25, 28, 34) and more than one of the paintings has been restored from descriptions and drawings preserved in the Cabinet des Dessins at the Louvre.

Vasari also says that Vignola was commissioned to design architectural *décors* for Primaticcio. This is a valuable piece of information; one often feels that the drawings are by two hands as the buildings are very precise while the figures are softer and more fluid. This collaboration seems likely in the *Diana* series of drawings which is now divided mainly between the Louvre and the École des Beaux-Arts. From the description by the Abbé le Blanc in 1753, it seems certain that they were intended as designs for windows at the Château of Anet which have since disappeared.

The School of Fontainebleau was the name given to a number of French and Italian painters who grouped themselves round Primaticcio. They refined on his sensuous charm but few of them possessed his talent. Among such artists as Fantuzzi, Thiry, or Penni, Niccolò dell'Abbate stands out. He was appreciated above all for his sense of colour but it is his large and brilliant pen drawings which show him to have been a supreme artist.

Félibien understood the part played by Primaticcio very well; "Primaticcio excelled in drawing and he employed many gifted men, with the result that an infinite number of drawings suddenly appeared in France better than anything seen before."

Among French artists of the time, there is the enigmatic Jean Cousin and the single drawing that we believe to be by him, or the decorative designer, Étienne Delaune, who drew tapestry cartoons and sketches for engravings. Then there is Antoine Caron. After years of neglect he is now recognized as one of the finest artists of the century. To please an exacting patron, Nicolas Houel, he made several series of drawings with elaborately worked detail; other freer drawings have also survived, sketches for paintings, studies in composition and studies of groups.

In the middle of the century, portrait drawings in chalk appeared again with François Clouet, the son of Jean Clouet. Like Primaticcio, he is one of the central figures in this book. His gifts compelled recognition in 1550 and for the next twenty years he dominated the artistic scene. His portraits were of kings and courtiers, although occasionally his sitters were more humble people. There are, for example, the all-too-rare drawings of artists such as Josset, Embroiderer to the King, or the portrait of the *bourgeoise,* Madame Liébaut.

Clouet was fortunate to find a firm admirer in Catherine de' Medici, the Queen-Mother. She loved drawings quite as much as paintings, and had acquired sketches by Jean Clouet. She made her painters copy and recopy those belonging to François Clouet, and no doubt kept her chalk drawings wrapped up in paper in chests like Queen Elizabeth I of England. She was an insatiable collector; Bouchot quotes a letter of hers to M. de Humières, Master of the Princesses' Household, with which she was sending portraits of "all her children, in chalk, to have more done" (15th June, 1552). Her beautiful mansion, the Hôtel de Soissons, was adorned solely with portraits.

This taste was shared by her family, particularly by her daughters whose marriages, arranged by their mother, took them far away. She left all her chalk drawings to one daughter, the Duchess of Tuscany. The other, who became Queen of Spain, had once been betrothed as a child of four to Edward VI of England. His portrait was hung in her room and she often stood in front of it and said to her mother: "I am saying good day to my lord, the King of England" (*State Papers*, vol. VIII, p. 249). At the age of eleven she sent Edward her portrait. It had been drawn, so she said, by one of her ladies-in-waiting whose name was Isabelle, the same as hers; according to the involved convention of the day this meant that she herself was the artist. Later on, in May 1559, her father sent Philip II a portrait of her by Marcantonio Sidonio the Venetian to assist in the marriage negotiations. Once in Spain she passed "her time in a whirl of portraits"; in 1561 she was helped by Sofonisba, "her great favourite", who used charcoal to draw from the life. Like her mother she employed portrait painters: Sanchez Coello was paid for "portraits and drawings" in 1563, in 1566 it was George de la Rua, "portrait painter", and in 1565 Esteban de Humotre, "French portrait painter", who may have been Étienne de Hamée.

In such circles as these where the chalk portrait drawing had pride of place, "Jannet" was considered by the Court to be the best portraitist in the world. Kings admired him and Catherine de' Medici used to watch him at work in his studio. In one recently published letter, Elizabeth, the young Queen of Spain, begs the French ambassador "to send her some good chalk drawings in every colour which she knows Jannet can do for her very skilfully". Ronsard called him "my Jannet", and considered him, somewhat generously, to be the equal of Michelangelo. Noblemen continually commissioned portraits from him. Baïf admired the milky whiteness of his faces which he emphasized by the delicacy of his finely drawn black line. He employed a whole studio of artists working in his style to meet the incessant demand.

The art of François Clouet had its limitations however; his faces are soft and unfailingly pleasant, they lack character and psychological insight. Even in the sixteenth century people noticed this; the Papal Nuncio remarked, about 1570, "that the French cannot paint what is really there", and that it would be difficult for him to send the Holy Father a portrait with any individuality. This note is curious and seems to show a new point of view; as A. M. Schmidt has shown, it coincides with Ronsard's instructions when he recommended physiognomy to the young Charles IX as being among the most necessary studies for a king, and also when he was showing up the weakness of a physiognomical analysis in 1569.

Despite their weaknesses, Clouet's drawings had a wide circulation. Groups of them were copied and are now known as the *Recueils de Seconde Main,* that is to say, sets of drawings of famous people at the French Court which private individuals ordered from his studio. About twenty have survived and it was once thought that they were drawn by the kings or nobles themselves. Now their mediocrity and generally commercial character is recognized. Clouet's drawings were also used in diplomatic negotiations; sent to foreign Courts they helped to make or mar treaties and royal marriages. In 1520 François de Montmorency had the task of reassuring Henry VIII as to the peaceful intentions of France and he brought with him drawings and presents (*"alcuni disegni e doni"* as the Venetian spies said). But the most curious episode took place between 1571 and 1574.

At that time there was some question of a marriage between Queen Elizabeth I of England and the Duc d'Anjou, later Henry III. The Queen commanded her ambassador to obtain a portrait of the Duke secretly so that she could see what he was like. On 15th February the ambassador announced that this could not be done; there was no way of getting hold of such a portrait for "no one is allowed to take a likeness of the King or his brother without permission; if they do the punishment is heavy". On 30th June despite renewed efforts he had to return to London empty-handed. However, he had asked officially for a portrait and on 3rd July Queen Catherine sent it to the French ambassador with a letter in which she said, "Master Jannet had no time, as you see, to do any more than the face which is very good and perfectly true to life", she also said that besides this one she had sent a full-length drawing although the face was unfinished: Clouet had not been "pleased" to "draw the face in detail because the other had been done, and I wanted to send off the messenger as quickly as possible". Both of them were to be given to the Earl of Leicester in the meantime and a large painting by Clouet would follow later. Sketches for these drawings are preserved in the Cabinet des Estampes, one for the portrait of the Duke standing (plate 60), and two for the head. The portrait, which was sent off on 3rd July, arrived in London on the 9th. The ambassador received it and wrote to Catherine on 28th July to say what he felt: he was somewhat disappointed and was afraid that Elizabeth would feel the same, for Clouet had not flattered his model; however, he continued, "although it is only a chalk drawing and his complexion is almost entirely covered in charcoal, his face shows much beauty and many signs of dignity and prudence". Elizabeth hesitated: the Duc de Nevers was pressing and warned her that the Duc d'Anjou "was unlucky in that no portraits did him justice, and that even Jannet himself had not given that admirable *je ne sais quoi* with which nature had endowed him". Before making up her mind Elizabeth decided to wait for a "life-size" portrait of the Duke "in colour". However, the marriage did not take place as Anjou had "too much respect for his religion". Catherine advised her ambassador (28th September, 1571) to put forward her youngest son, the Duc d'Alençon (he was seventeen years old and Elizabeth thirty-eight) but on this occasion she rejected the "trial by portrait", for the Duke, who had once been a delightful child, was now disfigured by smallpox. He was so frightful to look at that, when Cavalcanti brought a portrait of him to London in April 1572, the Tuscan Chargé d'affaires expressed lively fears.

Queen Elizabeth, on the other hand, was very reticent, six letters to the French ambassador speak only of the "inconvenience of his face". She was afraid that the "impediment" had given the Duke a double nose even worse than Clouet had drawn and thought up a complicated system for getting a more authentic likeness. She sent the English Postmaster-General, Randolph, to France and commanded him to take back the French portrait, he was to have a good look at the Duke, get a new portrait of him and bring that one back immediately. Charles IX received Randolph at La Fère and presented him to the Duke whom he found "quite different and much more pleasant" than he had expected. He brought back another portrait to London in a sealed box so that it could not be changed on the journey: in addition to these precautions the King sent a copy to his ambassador in England, La Mothe-Fénelon (5th December, 1573). This time the Queen seemed satisfied, everyone thought that the marriage would take place and Catherine de' Medici had already (5th February, 1574) provided for the "presents and gifts". But her letter crossed with one from La Mothe-Fénelon (3rd February, 1574) in London. He announced that Queen Elizabeth had decided against the marriage because she was really put off by the pock-marks which the portrait had shown on the young prince's face. On this occasion Clouet's fidelity had wrecked a scheme which would certainly have reunited France and England as one kingdom; the destiny of the two countries was altered by a single drawing.[1]

Besides Clouet, there are scattered references to many other portraitists. Their work has not survived although their contemporaries thought very highly of them; there was Jean Patin who at the age of fourteen was apprenticed to François Clouet to learn "the craft and merchandise" (that is to say, the art of painting portraits and the methods of selling them); Pierre Gourdelle, painter to Charles IX and *Valet de Chambre ordinaire* to the Queen-Mother, was friendly with Caron whose daughter Suzanne he married; Jean Rabel, of Beauvais, "one of the foremost in the art of portraiture" was asked by Guillaume Dupeyrat for a drawing of his lady:

> "Dépêche-toi Rabel, ce crayon désiré
> Des beautés de ma belle, et dépeins-moi sa grâce. . . .
> Haste-toi, mon Rabel, et fais que ce portraict
> Ainsi que je le veux, soit incontinent faict."

Nothing survives by Ronsard's friend, Denisot, who drew the *Fair Ladies* of all the *Pléiade*, scarcely anything by Boba, nothing at all by many others. There

[1] In January 1576, Henry III tried to reopen negotiations by sending a new portrait. Again in 1578 the Duke sent a "portrait of his exact size and stature" to the Queen who sent him a portrait of herself. G. Lebel was the first to realize the interest of this affair and we have had to piece together much scattered information. *Additions to the Memoirs of Castelnau*, vol. II, p. 361; vol. III, pp. 364, 387, 477; *La Mothe-Fénelon Correspondence*, vol. V, pp. 42, 44, 51, 54, 71, 74, 406; vol. VI, p. 22; *Crosby, 1573*, No. 1206; *Desjardins, Negotiations with Tuscany*, vol. III, p. 767: *State Papers, Venetian, 15 Nov. 1578*.

seem to be no surviving drawings by Corneille de Lyon and the whole of his studio has disappeared although he had several painter descendants right down to the eighteenth century. Jean Prieur of Amiens is known only by name although on his death in 1569 he left nineteen portraits; so is his relative Mathieu Prieur, who bequeathed to his family in 1619 "seven hundred portraits on paper, in chalk and roughly drawn, various portraits from the life, both men and women in different sizes".

On the other hand there are hundreds of drawings which do not seem to be by Clouet but which are difficult to ascribe; Bouchot, Dimier and Moreau-Nélaton have suggested names which, often wrongly, have not yet been accepted. The charming portrait of Mary Stuart in white mourning, one of the most famous drawings of the century, can be placed and dated (plate 56). It does not seem to be by Clouet and has been attributed several times to the only artist mentioned in accounts and inventories as being near the Queen at that time. He was a painter and embroiderer called Pierre Odry or Oudry whom Mary brought back with her to Scotland. But the artist might have been Jean Decourt who also worked for her. Jean Decourt was painter to Charles IX and, according to Papyre Masson, when the King was on his deathbed, he commanded him to bring a portrait of the young Henry III that he, Decourt, had painted. A drawing of the Lady Marshal of Retz in the Cabinet des Estampes can be ascribed to him. It is drawn conventionally enough but owing to the fame of the sitter it was highly praised by her friends (plate 85). Dimier groups a set of drawings round the so-called Painter of Luxembourg-Martigues; other portrait drawings, generally of Protestants, very dry and straightforward in style, can perhaps be attributed to Marc Duval.

After the deaths of Clouet and Primaticcio drawing changed its character; there had always been a division between portraits and mythical subjects but now the latter began to show signs of new life. Under the influence of Niccolò dell'Abbate not only architectural draughtsmen like Du Cerceau emerge, but also true landscape painters like Étienne Dupérac. He was one of the only *ruiniste* landscape artists of the time, perhaps because he was an architect and landscape gardener. At Venice he had engraved large coast views after drawings by the School of Titian, and he drew them himself. Paignon-Dijonval possessed "two views of Italian houses, another view of the sea-shore. . . , and a high rock with hermits' hovels at the foot and a cross on top". These drawings are "in pen and bistre wash heightened with white, on blue paper" and they are dated 1579 and 1580, that is to say about the end of Dupérac's time in Italy. A drawing in the British Museum shows his interest in the Villa d'Este where he may have worked on the lay-out of the grounds (plate 79).

The accession of Henry IV led to changes in the world of art. The old artists of the Court of Valois painted little after the Battle of Arques and the King's coronation; Caron was an old man and did not do much more before his death in 1599, neither did Étienne Du Moustier, who died in 1603; the pupils of Clouet degenerated into convention and mediocrity, the Italians disappeared and the last of the Fontainebleau painters confined themselves to the "custody" of old works.

A new train of artists appeared who had either been with the new King for some time, or who had stayed independent during the troubles of the League. For some years François Bunel, the son of another François Bunel, played an important part. He was born at Blois in 1550 and at the age of thirty, after working in obscurity at Tours, he became painter to the future Henry IV in succession to Duval; he painted portraits of the new King and the great men of his Court, and he had the honour of creating a new type, Henry IV with a short beard and brushed up hair, which was sent everywhere as a sort of official effigy. Bunel was certainly a gifted portraitist; he was obviously in the tradition of Clouet but he possessed the physiological and psychological insight which his predecessor had lacked. He did not work much in Paris and returned to Tours in 1590 where he died certainly before 1599. At the same time as Bunel the King undoubtedly employed Benjamin Foulon. He left Paris for Tours in 1589 where he remained until 1594. He was a mediocre artist who went on working until 1611. Both men followed the style of Clouet but the other portraitists in chalk were changing their style. Portrait drawing was dying from an excess of calligraphy, and it was the Quesnels, particularly the most gifted member of the family, Pierre (1543–1619), who introduced a more painterly approach. They used not only a clearer range of colours than Clouet and his school, but also flat washes to achieve broad modelling effects. This was something new and exceptional and the results are successful much more often than Dimier would allow. When the Court settled in Paris, one finds Du Moustier again, drawing portraits of the King and providing material for faithful engravers like Thomas de Leu.

The best portraitist of the day is known as the I.D.C. Master. Bouchot identifies him with Jean Decourt but his name will probably remain a mystery for many years yet. His drawings are delicious, the crowning achievement of the chalk portrait genre. His grand and sensitive style was unique in the century as the portrait of Gabrielle d'Estrées shows (plate 93). After this delightful portrait new developments in the art might have been expected; instead, paradoxically, 1599 was the year of its decline. I.D.C. was in fact an exception; there were plenty of artists drawing but they lacked his gift. To draw had become fashionable; children both in aristocratic and bourgeois families were taught drawing, especially portrait drawing, and they kept it up when they grew older. Jacques Antoine de Thou (1559–1617), for example, the great judge and one of the men who drafted the *Edict of Nantes*, could copy "engravings by Durer quite correctly" before he was ten years old. This taste and knowledge were not unusual in his family, his uncle Adrian and his brothers Jean and Christophe were equally gifted. When he was nineteen, in 1572, de Thou drew a portrait of the Baron des Adrets from memory which showed his wild air, his aquiline nose and his thin face covered with red spots. The following year on a diplomatic journey in Italy with Paul de Foix he admired the Italian painters, quoting Vasari whom he had read carefully (*Memoirs*, 1711, pp. 3, 9, 18, 34), and his lively talent decorated many pages of his memoirs. Another nobleman, Nicolas de Digne of Champagne, Sieur de Condes and Abbot of L'Enfourchure (*c.* 1560–after 1611), a pleasant and prolific poet, studied with Étienne Du Moustier, whom he praised very highly. There are many indications of his love of drawing, and his friend, the Sieur de la Couronne, liked his drawings as much as his poetry and watched him at work with some interest:

> "J'admire de ta main le labeur furieux
> Quand elle veut tirer une beauté nouvelle,
> Car ton subtil crayon la rend si naturelle
> Que le naturel même à peine semble mieux."

Le Digne himself wrote in his *Fleurettes* that

> "Songeant à mes amours, l'autre jour j'entrepris
> De crayonner les traits des beautés de ma dame."

Many more could be mentioned; Jean Bertaut, for example, the future Bishop of Sez, who was well known at the age of eighteen, in 1580, for his "strong and natural likenesses in pastel". When he wanted to become tutor to the Matignon family at Thorigny, he demonstrated his accomplishments by drawing the master of the house in coloured chalk (cf. Grente, *Bertaut*, 1903, p. 15). But the number and mediocrity of such drawings was their downfall, the public grew tired of them and engravings by men like Thomas de Leu and Léonard Gaultier were serious rivals.

However, even if portraiture had foundered in a sea of slickness and mediocrity, there were artists like Dubois, Dubreuil and Fréminet to save French drawing. They are called quite wrongly the Second School of Fontainebleau. They were very different from the School of the 1550's and did not form a homogeneous group. Toussaint Dubreuil had studied at the "School of M. de Saint-Martin"; he was a more gifted, more painterly Caron and he knew more than Caron about Italian painting. Blunt regards him as a link between Primaticcio and Poussin; he was a talented draughtsman and Van Mander wrote that when a picture was commissioned he followed the example of his forerunner and gave his designs to a *pléiade* of pupils who did the actual painting. Ambroise Dubois (the French name of Bosschaert, a native of Antwerp) had no connection with Dubreuil; he was a Mannerist in style and influenced by the engravings of

Spranger and Goltzius. These new masters were an important turning-point in French art; their style of painting and drawing marks the end of the sixteenth and the dawn of a new century.

Few sixteenth-century French drawings have survived. There are scarcely a thousand chalk portraits and this number is uncertain anyway owing to the confusion caused by two thousand mediocre copies; less than a thousand drawings by painters which are often little more than studio stock-in-trade, tracings or drawings by pupils; and perhaps three hundred ornamental and decorative designs —nothing compared with the quantities of eighteenth- or even seventeenth-century drawing. Moreover, the few that do exist are scattered among the various print rooms and libraries and this hampers research. There are many reasons for this scarcity, two in particular: disappearances that naturally occur over a long period of time, and attributions to the wrong artist. The latter is quite indisputable and any enquiring art historian can find numbers of sixteenth-century French drawings ascribed to the Italian School. But what of the disappearance of so many drawings? A few by Rosso have survived. He died without heirs and his property reverted to the King. He would certainly have sold the drawings—by that time out of fashion—in order to pay Rosso's debts, which were considerable despite his large salary. There is one drawing which may be by Jean Duvet, a few by Delaune, Jean Cousin, Du Moustier and Jean Goujon; Colombier does not mention one. Benvenuto Cellini says that in his hasty departure from Petit Nesle he had to leave behind his drawings and that in so doing he lost "the whole flower of my twenty years of study".

Only a few collections and albums of drawings are left. There are two collections of drawings by Antoine Caron which were commissioned by Nicolas Houel, doctor and patron; one is in the Louvre and the other in the Bibliothèque Nationale at Paris. One set of drawings by Du Cerceau, the architect, is in London, the other in Paris. Mariette draws attention to a "collection of drawings by Delaune, very large, done mainly with pen and wash on vellum". The Louvre has a fine collection of drawings by Primaticcio which has remained more or less intact since about 1625; at that date they belonged to Des Nœuds de la Noue when that "excellent collector" was Controller of Buildings. In this position he would have been able to acquire these drawings from d'Hoey or Ruggeri, Keepers of the Fontainebleau Paintings. After Des Nœuds they belonged to Jabach, Crozat, and then to the King. Mariette, who had the task of breaking up Crozat's precious collection, acquired other drawings which were added to Des Nœuds' original nucleus. These went either to Sir Thomas Lawrence (Woodburn brought them back to France and they passed to Destailleur, Clément and Chennevières), or to the Albertina, thanks to the Prince de Ligne. In the same way works by Niccolò dell'Abbate from the collection of Audran, another Keeper of Paintings, passed into the Stockholm collection. Apart from Des Nœuds' drawings Crozat had thirty-six other drawings attributed to Primaticcio. Twenty-five were acquired by Tessin, whose nephew, the Comte de Sparre, thought that they represented "a masquerade given by Francis I for Charles V"; this is also the opinion of B. Dalbäck who has studied the drawings at Drottningholm. The drawings done by Leonardo in France were bequeathed in his will to Francesco Melzi. They formed an album which was well known in Italy in the sixteenth century. It then passed to Pompeo Leoni, and through various hands until it was bought by Queen Victoria and Prince Albert.

Jean Clouet's drawings had an even more curious fate. Catherine de' Medici acquired them, no doubt through her favourite painter François Clouet about 1560, when he could say that he had been asked for more copies. These drawings had great sentimental value for the Queen-Mother. She had turned the memory of Francis I into a cult, and these were the portraits of people she had known at his Court in her youth. She made notes on them in her own handwriting, identified them from a very uncertain memory, as Bouchot has shown, and cherished them all her life. She left them to her grand-daughter in Florence, Christiane of Lorraine, who in 1589 found herself in possession of "a chest containing five hundred and fifty portraits of princes and princesses, lords and ladies". Interest in this chest of drawings waned during the seventeenth century and in 1736 it was put up for sale. Two Englishmen bought the collection, Ignazio Hugford and the Earl of Carlisle. Some of the portraits stayed in Florence, Hugford bound his thirty-two into an album, now in the British Museum, and Henry Howard, Earl of Carlisle (died 1758), kept his drawings, three hundred altogether, at Castle Howard. One of his descendants sold them in 1890 to the Duc d'Aumale and they are now at Chantilly. Those which stayed in Florence reappeared recently and are now divided between the Fogg Art Museum and the University Library at Harvard.

François Clouet's drawings passed neither to his own sons nor to his spiritual heir, Jean Patin, but to his nephew, the painter Foulon, who was ruthless in claiming his inheritance. By the beginning of the seventeenth century the studio estates of Duval, Quesnel and several other painters had been added to Foulon's collection. They all belonged to Jacques Dubouchet de Villeflix who, according to Bonaffé, may have acquired them from his wife. She was a member of the Elbène family who may have got the drawings from Pierre l'Estoille, but this is not absolutely certain. Villeflix marked his drawings "VX" or signed them and he did the same with several Jean Duvet prints which he also collected. It is likely that the next owner was the Abbé de Marolles, for in 1672 he had "many chalk drawings of the old Court . . . by the hand of François Jannet, the famous painter". He died in 1681 and Gaignières had them bound in five volumes which passed on his death in 1717 into the Bibliothèque du Roi.

Brisacier, another collector, sold his drawings in 1677; some were bought by an Englishman and are now in the Ashmolean Museum at Oxford, others were bought by Rousseau, Auditor of Accounts, who resold them to Lallemant de Betz. His collection entered the Cabinet des Estampes in 1753. The first President Achille de Harlay, who died in 1712, gave the collection, later the library, of Sainte-Geneviève "rare" drawings "in a generous and gracious way". In 1861 they were transferred to the Cabinet des Estampes whose *Conservateur* had bought in 1825 a parcel of fifty-seven portraits attributed to Jannet from the painter Lecurieux. They turned out to be Foulon's drawings from Clouet's estate. In this way the Bibliothèque Nationale acquired a unique collection of portraits from the second half of the century.

There is a superb and little known collection at the École des Beaux-Arts. Jean Masson, who had a passion for early French drawings, gave several boxes of sixteenth-century drawings forty years ago. This gift augmented an earlier set of drawings so that now the École des Beaux-Arts has a particularly rich collection.

In these various ways precious examples of French sixteenth-century drawing have been preserved. They are still too little known and this, the first book devoted entirely to them, has forced us to agree with Chateaubriand, who loved early drawings, when he said that for him "the great century of the arts" was the century of Francis I.

Finally, I should like to thank the following people for their invaluable help: Anthony Blunt, Director of the Courtauld Institute of Art; Agnes Mongan, Keeper of Drawings at the Fogg Art Museum; Otto Benesch, Director of the Albertina and Werner Hofmann, Keeper; Philip Pouncey, Keeper at the British Museum; Bengt Dalbäck, of the Stockholm Museum and Jean Ehrmann. I am very much indebted to Madame Bouchot-Saupique, who has always made me welcome at the Cabinet des Dessins at the Louvre, for allowing me to draw so freely on the research of her father, the late Henri Bouchot. I am equally indebted to the researches of the following scholars: Louis Dimier, Pierre Lavallée, Lebel, Du Columbier, and Gébelin.

JEAN ADHÉMAR

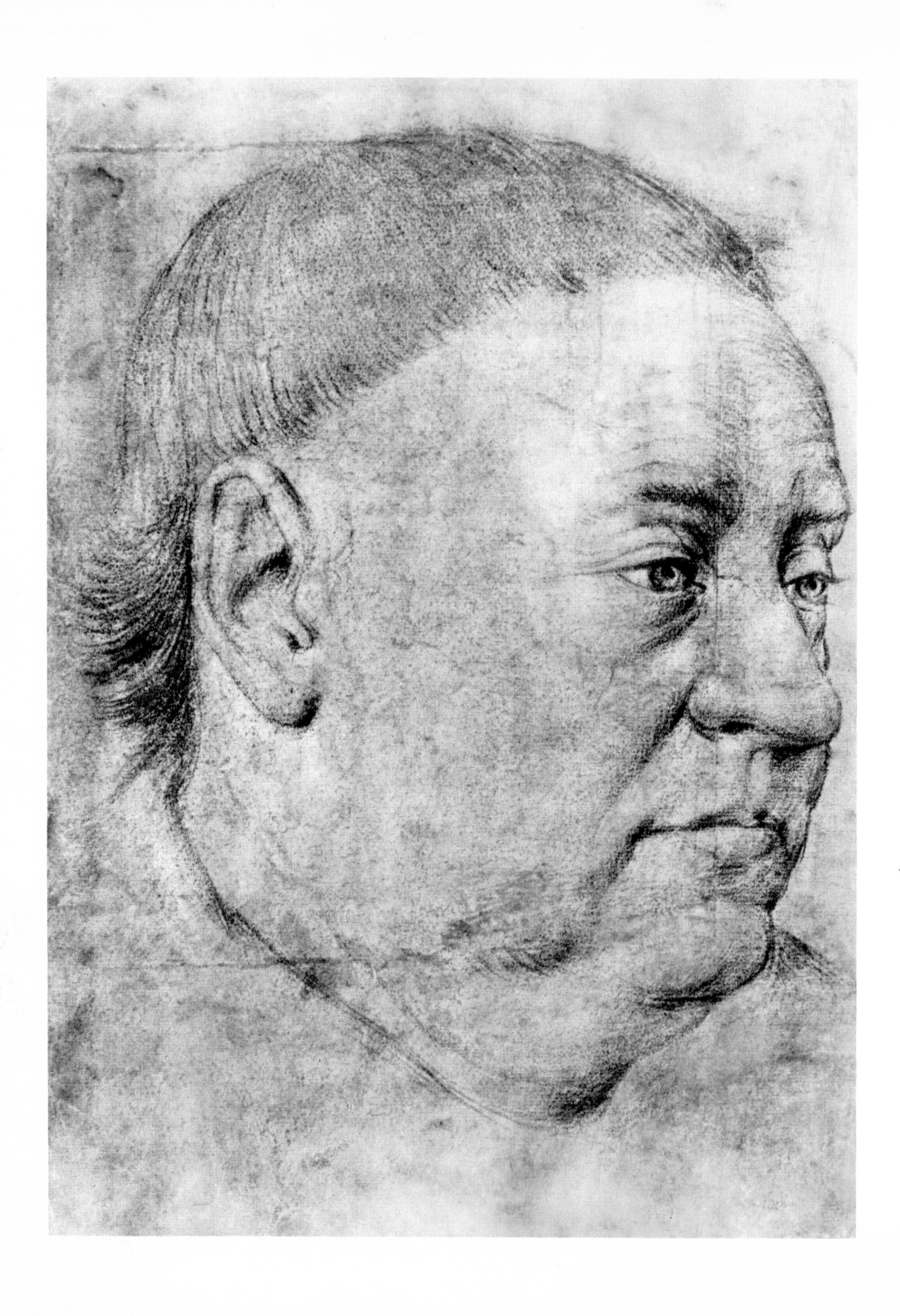

LE ROY RENE
De prouuece

216

173

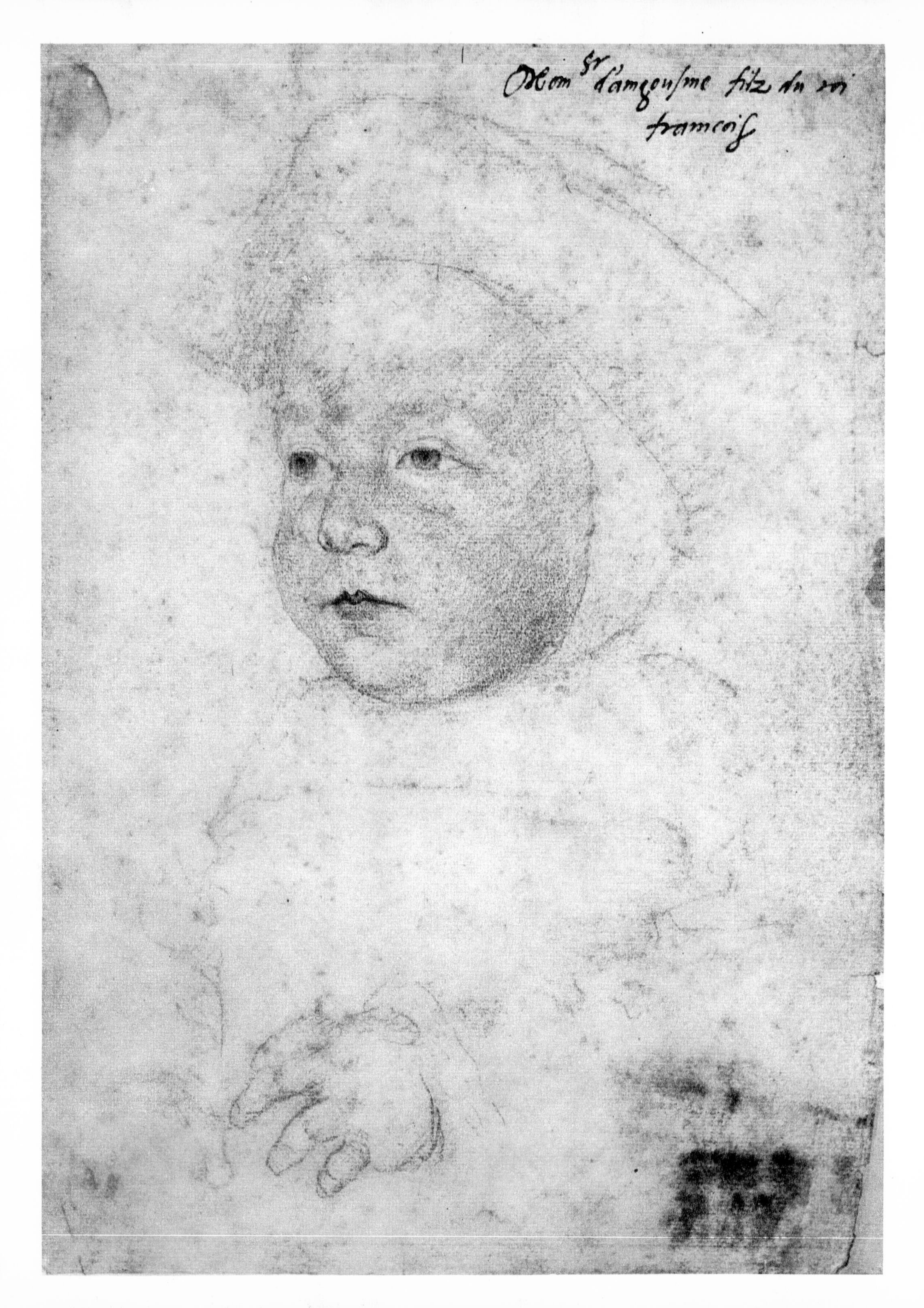
Monsr d'angousme filz du roi
francois

La Balliue de Cam

Çapata

la feu roine de nauarre
marguerite

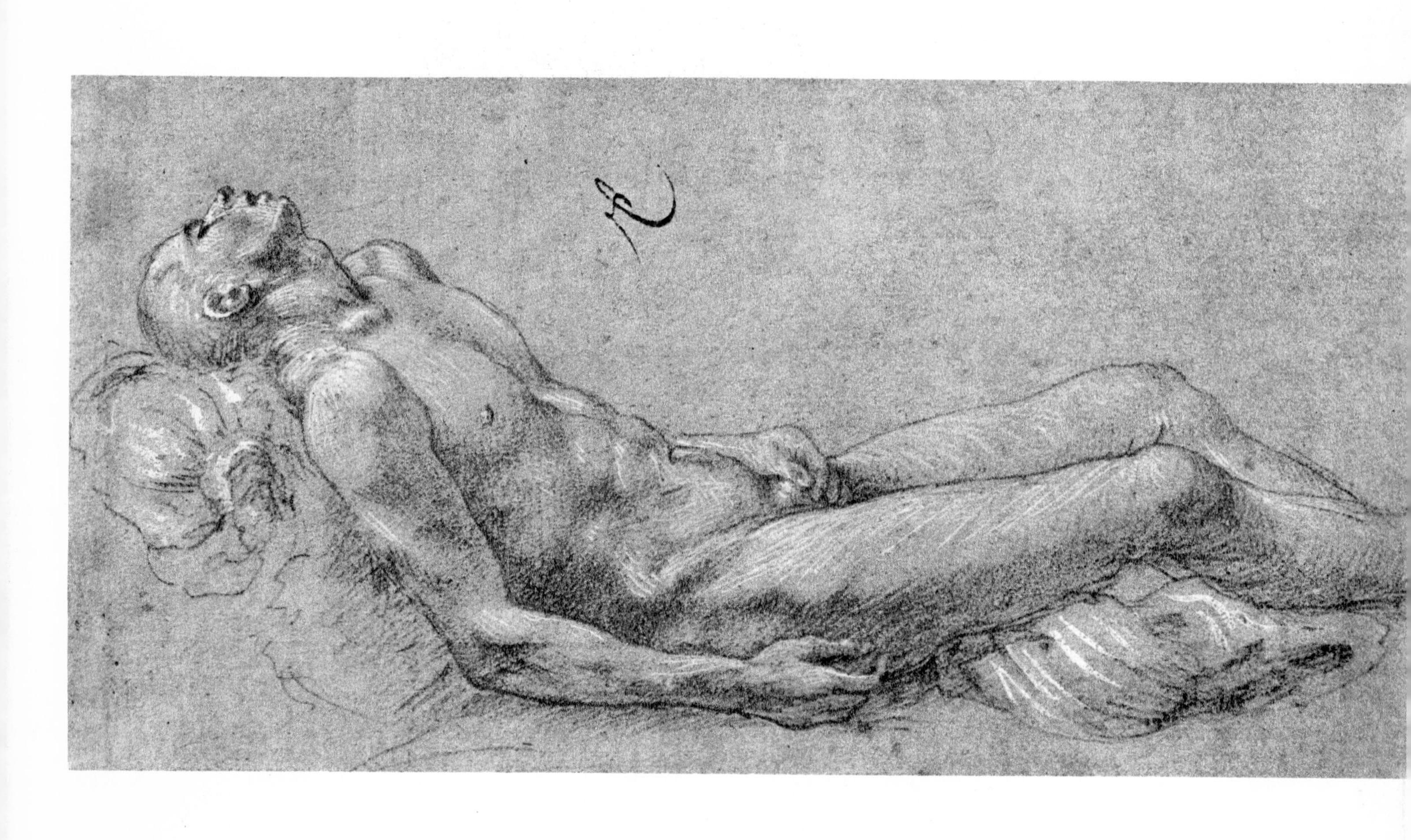

Armoyrye timbree
Armoyrye D Madame
D O M
Basse taille
C M

primatris.
12

Bologne fecit

Tiboulet

J. Cousin

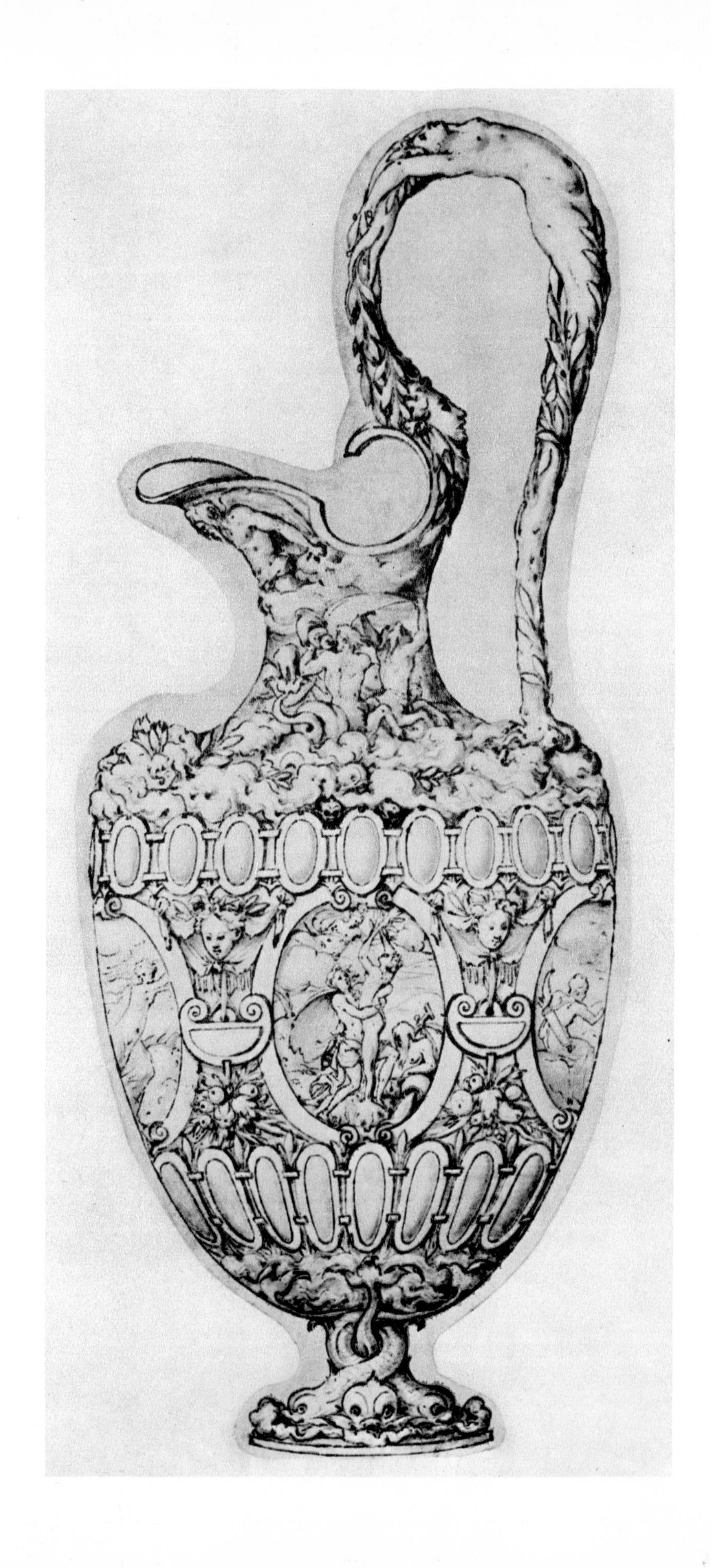

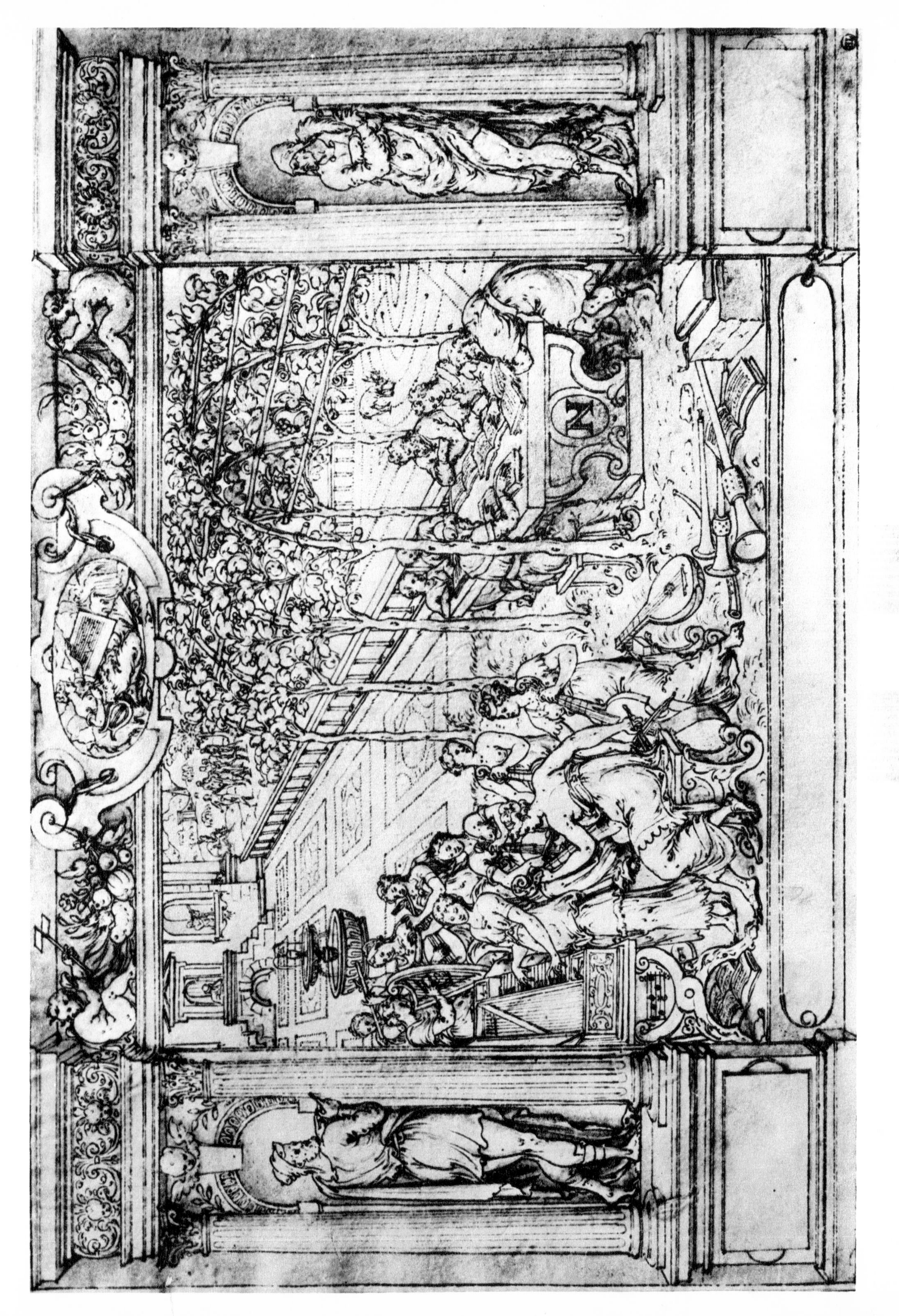

ce dessin est dans la manière de Jacques
Voy. ci devant pag. 45.

Madame de Savoye estant Mdme Marguerite

Le gran Roy
francois

La Duchesse de Valentinoi

Charles IX. En leage de 12 ans

Marguerite Duchesse de Valois 3.me fille de Henry II. née le 14. May 1551. mariée
le 18. aoust 1572: à Henry IV.
morte le 27. mars 1615.

la roine mere du ro

24
Marie Stuart

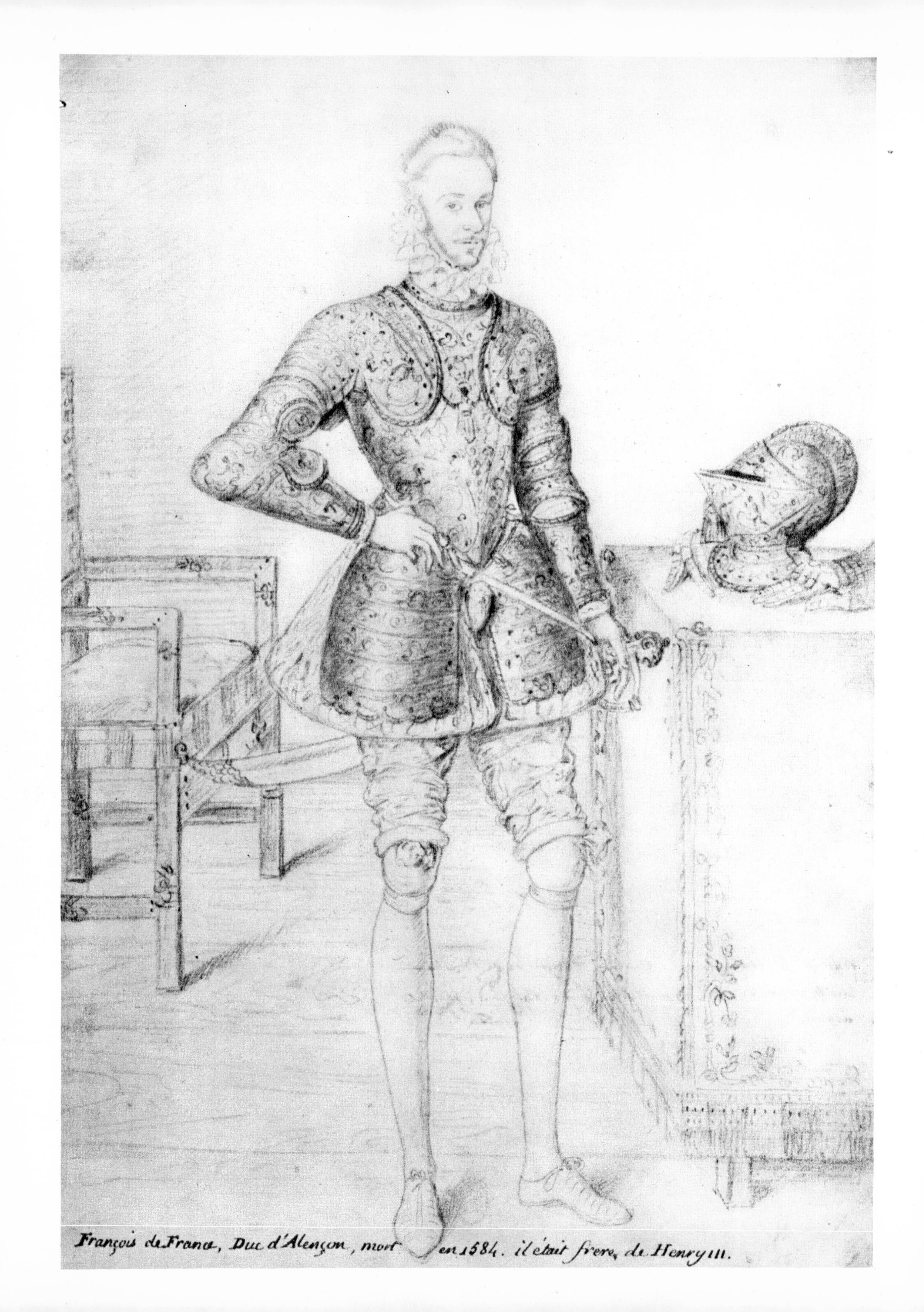
François de France, Duc d'Alençon, mort en 1584. il était frere, de Henry III.

Pierre Du Monstier.
Estienne Du Monstier laisné.
La Royne Mère du Roy.

ARDOREM
TESTANTVR
EXTINCTA
VIVERE FLAMMA.

ARDOREM
TESTANTVR
EXTINCTA
VIVERE FLAMMA

ARDOREM
TESTANTVR
EXTINCTA
VIVERE FLAMMA.

ARDOREM
TESTANTVR
EXTINCTA
VIVERE FLAMMA.

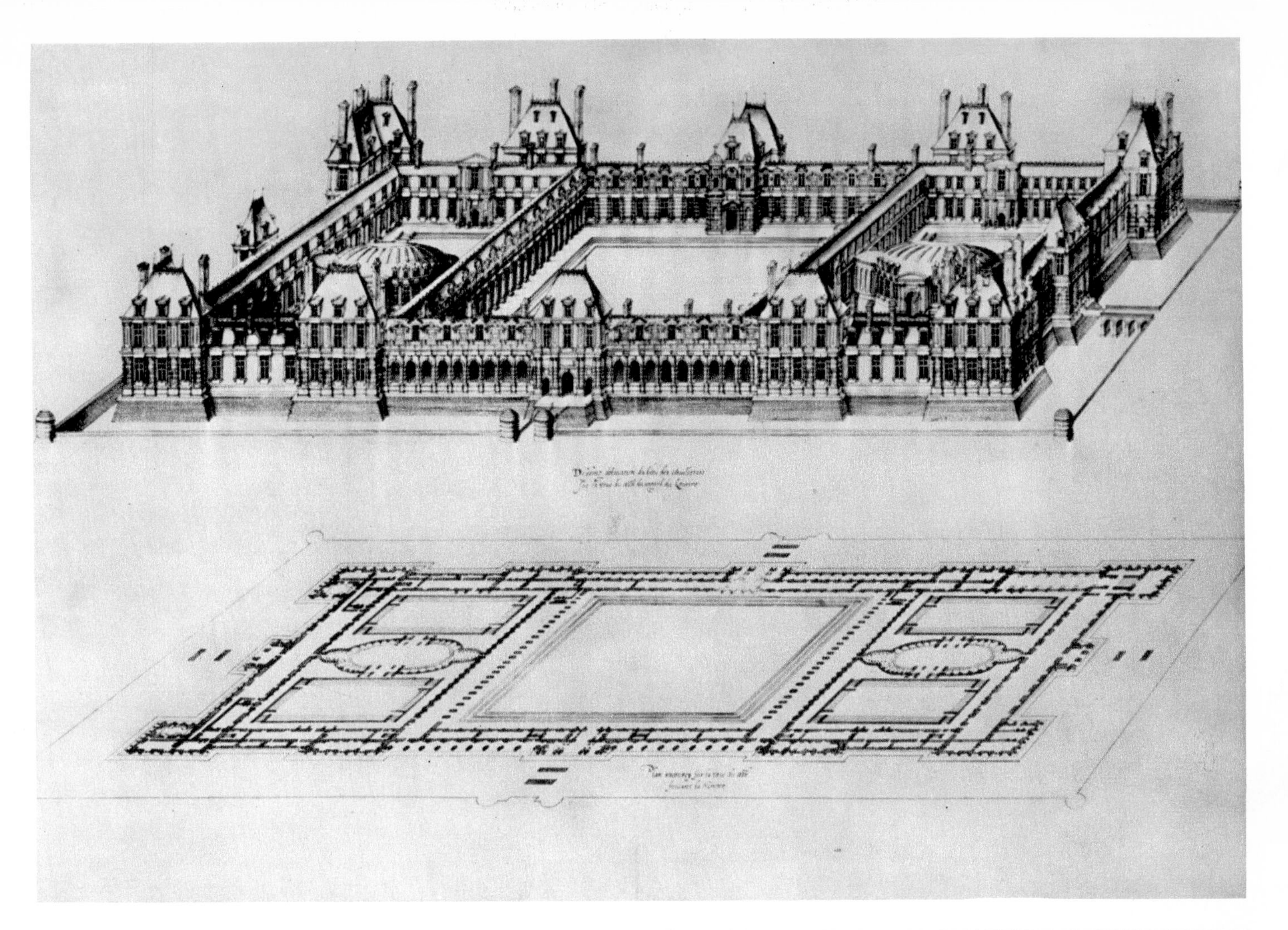

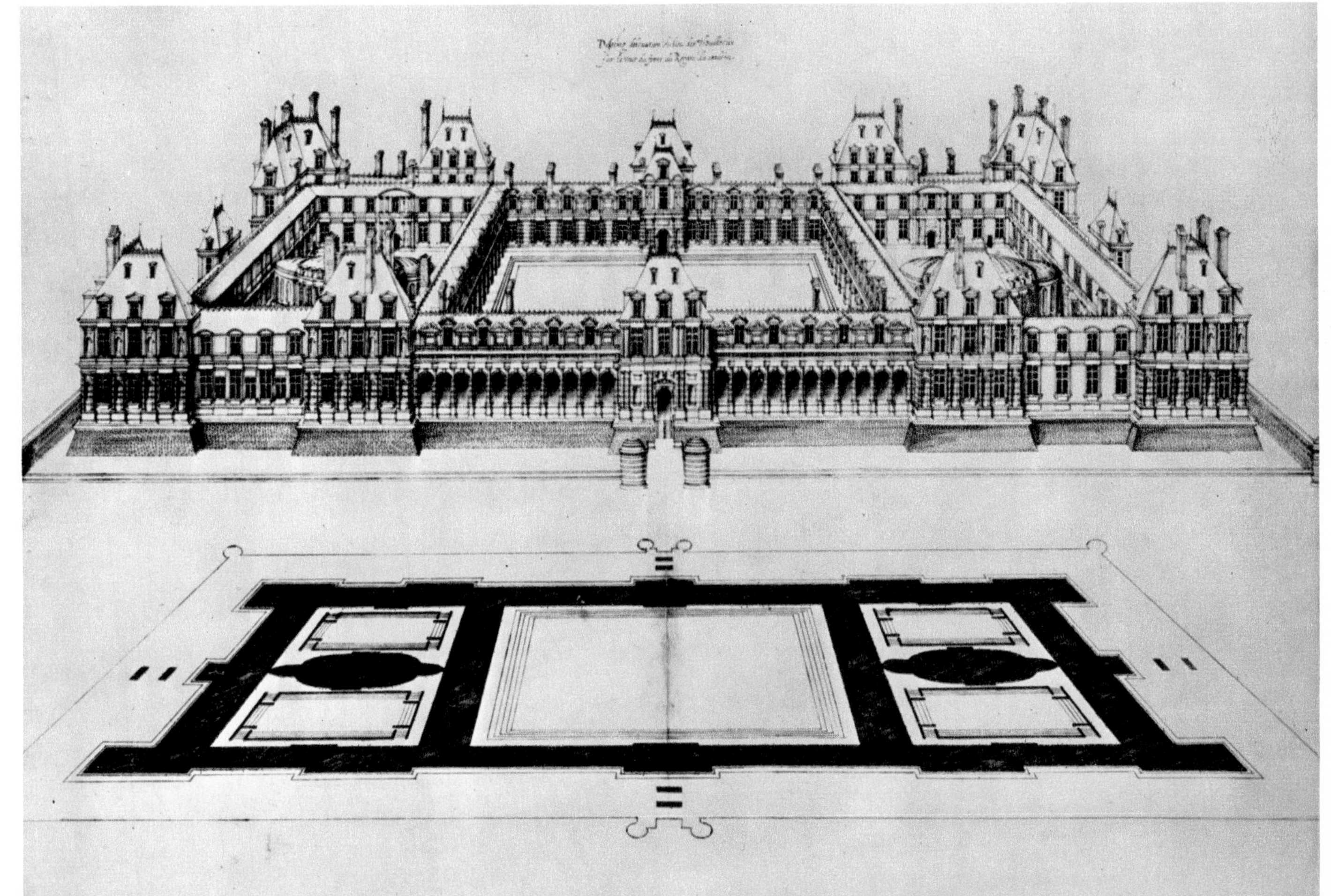

Bele pare
909

Beauveau de
Tremblecour
Louis de Beauvau seign. de Tremblecourt mort en 1596.

Parmezan

Mr de Sully surintendant.
Maximilien de Bethune Duc de Sully, mort en 1641.

Me fecit
1600

BIOGRAPHICAL NOTES

BIOGRAPHICAL NOTES

LEONARDO DA VINCI

1452–1519

Leonardo's French period, which is all we shall consider here, is preceded by a highly characterized Milanese period, lasting from 1506 to 1513. These dates, as Professor Blunt has pointed out, coincide with a time when Milan was under French rule. When this happened, Leonardo automatically became painter and engineer to the King of France, Louis XII, who referred to him as "*notre cher et bien aimé*" and asked him to send some of his works to France. Leonardo seems to have been quite attached to him and made a note of the date of his death.

In December 1515 he was apparently instrumental in the meeting of Francis I and Leo X at Bologna, and was probably presented to the new King who invited him to make his home in France.

He left Italy at the end of 1516 and arrived in France at the beginning of the following year. It was not, however, until the 14th May, 1517 (he notes the date) that he settled at the Château of Cloux, which the King had prepared for him.

The King loved to discuss art, philosophy and mathematics with him, so much so, say contemporaries, that he stopped him from working (by which they mean painting). At the King's command, he constructed mechanical devices for a fête which took place on 30th September at Argentan where Francis I went to meet his sister Marguerite, Duchesse d'Alençon, whose wit and beauty, according to Michel François, made her "the true Queen of France". Twelve lords, each with a German or Italian lady, took part in a tourney. The King won and was presented by a hermit with a wand; with this he rapped three times on the body of a lion which opened up to reveal fleurs-de-lis on a bed of azure. According to a letter of Rinaldo Ariosto, all this was "the Duchess's own invention".

On the following day Montmorency arrived on this scene of royal pleasure with another device, this time a golden heart which opened to show a Cupid, with his body divided into two: on one side a child clad in armour, on the other a child naked and weeping. This was an allegory of *Favour and Displeasure*.

The fête ended on the 10th October and the King left Argentan for Moulins. It would therefore be difficult to accept this date for the famous visit to Cloux of the Cardinal of Aragon; Italian scholars consider that it took place in 1518.

In January 1518, Leonardo was at Romorantin supervising the first stages of the carrying-out of his revolutionary plan for the château, which included things like pre-fabricated lodgings for the courtiers and a canal for water tourneys. He worked on a system of canals linking Romorantin, Tours, Amboise, Blois and Lyons, to facilitate the royal journeys in that region and in the direction of Italy.

In May he organized the fêtes given at Amboise for the marriage of Lorenzo de' Medici and Madeleine de la Tour d'Auvergne (the future parents of Catherine de' Medici), and which also celebrated the baptism of the Dauphin. A tiltyard was set up in the square with a triumphal arch surmounted by a huge painted column. The fête, which took place on the 16th May, consisted of a battle to commemorate the Victory of Marignano. The King, wearing cloth-of-gold, was once again victorious.

On the 19th June Leonardo organized another fête at Cloux. The courtyard of the château was covered with sky-blue parchment decorated with gold stars and planets, and surrounding columns were spangled with stars. We do not know what the entertainment consisted of, but a costume drawing of a prisoner which has come down to us is probably connected with it. It has been stated, but with no supporting evidence that this fête was a repetition of one organized by Leonardo in Milan in 1490.

Leonardo made a note of the date 24th June in his papers but its significance is not known.

On the 10th October he was visited by the Cardinal of Aragon whose secretary Antonio de Beatis notes that Leonardo showed him three pictures, a *Portrait of a Lady*, a *St John the Baptist*, and a *Holy Family*. He added that Leonardo was no longer able to do anything more than draw, that he showed them a treatise on anatomy on which he was working, and finally spoke of his engineering projects.

Leonardo fell ill on the 23rd April, 1519. On the 2nd May he died in the arms of Francis I.

Technically Leonardo's French drawings are quite different from his Italian ones and are therefore easy to recognize. They were in fact collected by Melzi and made into an album, now at Windsor, from which the drawings reproduced in this book have been taken.

The above information, which is not generally found in French monographs on Leonardo, is taken largely from a very important article by E. Salmi, "Documenti inediti, sulla demora di Leonardo in Francia", published in *Archivio Storico Lombardo, Ann.* 31, 1904, pp. 388–410.

JEAN CLOUET

about 1475/80–1541

Son of another Jean Clouet, called Clouet of Brussels, who was in France in 1475, 1480 and perhaps 1485. Born like his father in Brussels (or possibly at Tours according to Laborde), he became a member of the Royal Household on the accession of Francis I and succeeded Bourdichon in 1523 as *Valet de Garde-Robe extraordinaire*. He worked in Tours, where he married a silversmith's daughter, Jeanne Boucault. His fame grew, he became rich, and in 1522 he bought from his relative Fichepin, probably also a silversmith, jewels for which he paid the enormous sum of 80 *écus*. The following year his wife sold their house, which consisted of two main buildings and two courtyards, in Clouet's absence. He had left Tours for Paris, where he became Painter and *Valet de Chambre ordinaire* to the King earning a salary of 240 *livres* a year. In addition to these appointments he received gifts of money and livery (in 1525 he sold four Court dresses for 40 *écus d'or*).

There is in existence a document which identifies him as the painter of a portrait of Budé. On the basis of similarity of style, a number of chalk drawings at Chantilly have been attributed to him.

His name appears several times in the Royal Accounts, notably in 1529, when the King sent him "post-haste" to Paris to collect some portraits and bring them back to Blois. Similarly, in 1537, his wife travelled from Paris to Fontainebleau to show the King "some works by the said Jehannet". In 1533 he was Court Painter and *Valet du Roi*, while his assistant Petit-Jean Champion (who had been working with him since 1525) was only *Valet de Garde-robe*. He died in November 1541.

JEAN DE GOURMONT THE ELDER

about 1483–1551

Painter and engraver, born at Carquebut (Manche) about 1483; died in 1551. He was a brother of Robert and Gilles de Gourmont, the great Parisian printers, with whom he worked in Paris until 1520. He then settled in Lyons and became a member of the Lyons School which, according to documents, was extremely active in the sixteenth century but of which very little has survived. Gilles, his nephew and probably his pupil, engraved book illustrations in Paris until about 1596.

JEAN COUSIN

about 1490–about 1560

Painter, born in Sens of a wealthy family of merchants, possibly silversmiths, which counted a canon in its ranks. Towards 1520 he married Christiane Rousseau, also from a well-to-do family of merchants, tax-collectors and clerics. This explains why Cousin, who never held a Court appointment (he does not figure in the Fontainebleau Accounts) was looked upon by contemporaries as a man of considerable substance. Until 1540, mentions of him in contemporary documents are scarce but those that exist hint at a certain importance and esteem. Like other painters, Cousin was employed by the town of Sens as a surveyor (1526), he painted an important altarpiece for the Abbey of Vauluisant (1530), and he designed stained-glass windows for the Cathedral (about 1530–42).

He settled in Paris in or around 1540, the year of Rosso's death and Primaticcio's return. He died about 1560. We have documentary evidence for a certain number of commissions during these twenty-odd years: in 1541 he made tapestry cartoons of the life of St Genevieve, and about 1550 designed ecclesiastical ornaments for the Cathedral of Sens. A wealthy man, Cousin bought a large plot of land in the rue de Seine, and made a great show of financial independence. Du Colombier interprets his refusal to pay court to the stingy nobility as "the gesture of a competent painter in easy circumstances who preferred to work for the merchants and bourgeois, who paid better and more promptly". Since the time of Papillon (*Traité de la gravure sur bois*, 1766, vol. I, p. 202) it has been customary to attribute to Cousin a number of illustrated books, such as the *Orus Apollo* of 1543 and others mentioned by R. Brun and Robert-Dumesnil.

Contemporary sources tell us little of Cousin's private life. All we know is that his brother-in-law was Aubin Olivier, the medallist and engraver, that his wife's half-brother was Jacques Couste the painter who after 1560 worked with Caron, that he had a son, Jean the Younger, who was also a painter, as well as several daughters who married armourers or locksmiths, whose sphere is close to that of engravers on copper.

Maurice Roy, to whom we owe the greater part of our knowledge of Cousin, claims (but with no supporting evidence) that his large house in Paris contained a studio for pupils and a classroom. It is, in any case, certain that he was considered a great man in his own lifetime. Vasari mentions him in 1550; while Le Roy in 1575, Le Fèvre de la Boderie in 1578 and Jean des Carres in 1581 speak of him in the same breath as Durer, Alberti and Caron.

We know that one of his most notable works was his share in the *Entry of Henry II into Paris* (1549). He and the Fontainebleau artist, Dorigny, were in charge of the paintings while Goujon was responsible for the architecture and sculpture. All were under the direction of the theorist, Jean Martin. Historians give no account of the finished pictures although they were important and would go a long way to define his style and the models he set himself. This was the programme he carried out at the Porte Saint-Denis: a triumphal arch in *trompe l'œil* supported by two rustic giants and surmounted by four figures symbolizing the Four Estates. The four figures were linked by a golden chain passed through their ears and held by a "Gallic Hercules" symbolizing Francis I, by whose eloquence they were subdued.

In front of Saint-Jacques-de-l'Hôpital there was another triumphal arch for which he had painted two large pictures: on one side, the Seine crowned with laurel, leaning on a hydra and wielding an oar, and on the other, the Marne in similar style.

Finally, for the decoration of the Pont Notre-Dame, he painted several mythological scenes, notably two reclining figures done with artificial lighting effects: the nymph Aurora sitting on dark clouds, leaning on a bucranal mask, and holding a lamp, as a pendant to a still glowing Hesperus asleep on the clouds.

The reclining figures in the tradition of Primaticcio, Cellini and Jean Goujon and the chiaroscuro effects confirm the attribution to Jean Cousin of the Louvre *Eva Prima Pandora*, extremely close in style to his *Aurora*. The picture can, in fact, be traced to his family.

The traditional view of Jean Cousin as the teacher and guiding spirit of a whole generation of artists is, if anything, upheld by his treatises on *Perspective*, published in 1560 (but nearly completed by 1533), and the unfinished *Livre de Portraiture*, published by his son (in 1571, according to some). These two works were extremely successful; as early as 1561 Plantin sent a copy of the first to Jerome Cock in Antwerp, while the second was reprinted in 1589 and 1594, and there were at least twenty-four editions between 1594 and 1788.

Several engravings after Cousin should be also considered as models, notably a *Descent from the Cross*, a *Conversion of St Paul* (various expressions of terror), a *Brazen Serpent*, engraved by Étienne Delaune about 1560–69 (violent attitudes and *contrejour* effects), and a *Forge of Vulcan*, engraved by Léonard Gaultier in 1581 (a study of the nude and more violent attitudes). With these engravings as a guide, it should be possible one day to form a corpus of drawings by Cousin.

ROSSO
(Giovan Battista di Jacopo di Gasparro)
1495–1540

Painter, born in Florence. His early years are unknown; he enrolled as a painter in 1518 and in 1521 executed the curious highly-coloured *Descent from the Cross* at Volterra. In 1522–23 he was in Florence, and in 1524 in Rome in contact with Michelangelo, Mazzola and Caraglio who engraved his drawings. After the Sack of Rome, which ruined Rosso as it did most artists, he spent a difficult time in Northern Italy until 1529 when he met a kindred spirit, Pietro Aretino. Aretino commissioned from him a drawing representing *Mars brought to Venus by Cupids and the Graces*, an allegorical reference to Francis putting an end to the war by marrying Charles V's sister. Knowing Rosso's desire to live in France, Aretino sent the drawing to the King, who was delighted with it and invited the artist to make his home in Paris.

Rosso arrived in France in October 1530. In November the King commissioned a *Leda* (the picture, a copy of Michelangelo's *Leda*, is now in the National Gallery, London). In May 1532, the King accorded him certain privileges; in August he was made Canon of the Sainte-Chapelle. In 1532–34, he began his work on the decoration of Fontainebleau with the *Pavillon de Pomone*, in which he was assisted by Primaticcio. He worked on the *Galerie François I* from 1534–37.

He painted a *Judith* for the King and the Louvre *Pietà* for Constable Anne de Montmorency; he designed masquerades, fêtes (notably for the *Entry of Charles V* with

Primaticcio); he made drawings for silversmiths; he directed a team of Florentine and French painters which included Léonard Thiry, and he worked in conjunction with Scibec de Carpi, the decorative sculptor and wood-carver.

He died in November 1540. According to Vasari, two cartoons were found in his studio, a *Leda* and an *Augustus* to whom the Sybil reveals the Virgin. This is an extremely puzzling statement. The *Augustus and the Sybil,* which included "King Francis, the Queen, the army and the people, so many figures so well painted that one would be justified in calling it one of Rosso's finest works" is apparently the well-known painting by Caron in the Louvre, while we know that the King acquired the *Leda* in 1532. It seems likely that Vasari was mistaken.

At any rate Rosso, tall, distinguished, talented and well-read, "serious and of great discernment", the friend of Michelangelo and Aretino, was responsible for the introduction of Mannerism into France, together with a distinctive style of painting and, above all, of draughtsmanship. Unfortunately, his drawings (pen-and-wash, stump, chalk) are extremely rare.

FRANCESCO PRIMATICCIO

about 1504–1570

Painter, decorator and architect, born in Bologna. At the age of twenty-two he worked as Giulio Romano's chief assistant on the decoration of the Palazzo del Tè. It was as a decorator that Francis I invited him to France in 1532. He left Mantua between the 23rd January and the 23rd March, 1532, and arrived at Fontainebleau some time in April. The King was absent and did not return until 1534; it seems likely, therefore, that Primaticcio went to Paris to do homage.

He worked with Rosso, who entrusted him with the decoration of the *Pavillon de Pomone* in the garden, the *Porte Dorée* and the King's own room.

In February 1533 the King sent him to Flanders. In 1534 he sent him off again, with a grant of 200 *écus,* to take a small drawing of Scipio Africanus for "the tapestry which the King was having woven in Brussels and to bring back the large one". (This negotiation was begun on the 9th July, 1532.) In Brussels he competed with Antoine de Hollande for a commission from Ferdinand of Portugal.

In 1539 and 1540 he was responsible for the restoration of the Raphaels in the King's collection. On the 13th February, 1540, he took his leave of the King at Doullens and, at his behest, left for Rome. He brought back 133 cases full of works of art (125 antique sculptures, numerous statues, busts, torsoes, casts of the Laocoön, etc.). He also brought back Vignola and the bronze worker, François Ribon.

His return, hastened by the death of Rosso in November 1540 can be dated some time in the winter of 1541. From 1542–45, with the assistance of a team of painters, a large number of whom came from Bologna, he executed a "staggering" number of works (the word is Dimier's). He finished the King's room at Fontainebleau (1545), decorated the *Chambre d'Alexandre* (finished 1543), the vestibule of the *Porte Dorée* (1544), the *Grotte des Pins* (1543) and other rooms in the Palace. Most important of all, he decorated the *Galerie d'Ulysse*. He restored and arranged the antique statues and had bronzes made from the casts. He also directed a tapestry manufacture. Primaticcio became *Directeur des Beaux-Arts*; he made drawings which his pupils squared up and converted into the many decorative paintings which he was expected to produce. In 1544 the King made him Titular Abbot of Saint-Martin de Troyes. He also received many commissions from private patrons.

NICCOLÒ DELL'ABBATE

about 1512–1571

Painter, born in Modena. According to early biographers, he began life as a soldier and turned to painting in 1537 at the age of twenty-five. He became assistant to Alberto Fontana and retained this position until 1546, by which date he had become one of the most important painters in the studio. In 1547 he was working on his own in and around Modena and in Bologna.

In 1552 he was summoned to France, where he began by painting portraits of the King and the Dauphin (the future Francis II). For these he received a gold chain and the considerable salary of a 1000 *écus* per year. On the road to prosperity, he sent for his wife and children to join him.

He became Primaticcio's favourite assistant and supplied him with ideas for the Ballroom (painted in rich, melting colours, according to Vasari), for the *Chambre de Saint-Louis*, the *Chambre d'Alexandre*, and for the last part of the decoration of the *Galerie d'Ulysse*.

Many of his works, notably the illusionist decoration of the Hôtel de Guise (1555) are known to us only through documents or copies. About this time, he made his début as a painter of easel pictures, showing a feeling for landscape which Clouet, Rosso, and even Primaticcio practically ignored.

In 1561 he was once more at Fontainebleau, decorating the *Laiterie* with grotesques and the *Chambre du Roi* with landscapes. He also worked for private patrons, and produced a series of children's games for the Hôtel de Montmorency and decorations based on Ovid's *Metamorphoses* for Le Tellier.

It is difficult to isolate his work from that of Primaticcio, who was quite clearly influenced by his younger and more talented colleague. It is for this reason, and for the fact that they worked together, that so little mention is made of him. He did however come into his own on the death of Primaticcio when his son, Camillo dell'Abbate, succeeded the latter as *Surintendant des Peintures du Roi* at a salary of 400 *livres* per annum. (He in his turn was succeeded in 1580 by Ruggeri.) Niccolò's name is last mentioned in 1571 in connection with the restoration of a *Reclining Woman* by Titian in the Royal Collection, which has since disappeared, and for having prepared the King's entry into Paris. All the documents refer to him as "the first painter in Europe".

In 1546 he left for Rome in the company of Domenico Fiorentino and Vignola, with orders to bring back works by Michelangelo.

On the death of Francis I in 1547, Niccolò was for a time overshadowed by Philibert Delorme, who was more popular at Court. In any case renewed warfare had put a stop to large-scale projects. He therefore undertook work for private patrons, especially the powerful Guise family, and it was no doubt due to their influence that he obtained *Lettres de Naturalité* for his nephews in 1552. By that date he was back at Fontainebleau working on the Ballroom.

Henry II had allowed himself to be prompted by Diane de Poitiers' preference for Philibert Delorme, but when he died in 1559, Niccolò regained the protection of the Queen-Mother and the office of *Surintendant des Beaux-Arts*. With Caron and Primaticcio he completed the decoration of the *Galerie d'Ulysse*, was invested with the offices of *Conseiller du Roi* and *Aumônier de la Cour*, and organized the festivities celebrating the arrival of Francis II and his young Queen at Chenonceaux, Catherine de' Medici's new domain. He also directed the building of the Valois memorial at Saint-Denis and the monument for the heart of Francis II (1560).

In addition to these enormous programmes, he constructed the *Belle Cheminée* wing in the Fountain Court at Fontainebleau. He began this work in 1565 after a journey in 1563 to Bologna, where, as Blunt points out, he saw the works of his former assistant, Vignola.

He died in 1571, some time between the 15th May and the 14th September. His son Camillo succeeded him as *Surintendant des Peintures* but no one took his place as Director of the Fine Arts.

CORNEILLE DE LYON

about 1515–after 1574

According to Florent Fels (*Amour de l'Art*, September 1925), Corneille de Lyon was born at The Hague and his real name was Claudius-Cornelis van de Capelle. Without being quite so definite, we can safely say that the artist's real name should be Corneille de la Haye (Cornelis of The Hague). He was almost certainly Dutch by birth and born about 1515. By 1540 he was in Paris, holding the office of Painter to the Dauphin (the future Henry II, then twenty-two and married to Catherine de' Medici since 1533).

In 1544 he was in Lyons and known as Corneille the painter, or Corneille the Flemish painter. In Paris he had no doubt been overshadowed by Clouet's success. In 1545, his royal appointment, which he retained, enabled him to gain exemption from the wine tax from the Lyons Consulate. In 1547 his former master became King of France and granted him naturalization papers for "he came to live in our kingdom, married here, and wishes to remain here". At the same time the King made him Painter in Ordinary, although he never returned to Paris. In 1548 Stradanus spent six months in his studio (compare Borghini's *Riposo*). In September 1551, the Venetian ambassador, Giovanni Cappello, who was passing through Lyons, "paid a visit to an excellent painter who showed him not only many fine pictures but small life-like portraits of all the ladies and gentlemen of the French Court". Thus before leaving Paris Corneille had used his royal appointment to paint all the important people of the day; he kept the originals on show in his gallery in Lyons and made copies of them for sale.

In 1564 his gallery was visited by the King of Spain (compare Laborde, *Renaissance des Arts*, vol. I, p. 312). In the same year, according to Brantôme, Catherine de' Medici, on the occasion of a visit to Lyons, was enchanted to see in her room "all the nobles, princesses, ladies-in-waiting of the Court of France" (*Works*, ed. Lalanne, vol. X, p. 42). In 1569 "the painter Corneille de Lyon" was described as converted to the Church of Rome. In 1574 his privileges as Painter and *Valet de Chambre* to the King were recognized by the City of Lyons.

He had a daughter who "painted divinely" and a son, Corneille, who was also a painter. The latter had a son, Christophe de la Haye (called Me Corneille), who is mentioned in documents between 1591 and 1622. He in turn produced two sons and five grandsons, all painters. The last member of the dynasty died in 1706.

Spranger and Stradanus worked in the studio of Corneille de Lyon (to whom Van Mander refers as Cornelio del Aia).

FRANÇOIS CLOUET

about 1516/20–1572

Famous portrait painter, born in Tours, died in Paris. He stayed in Tours with his father until 1523, then went with him to Paris, and succeeded him at his death in about 1541. At this time he acquired the title of Painter to the King, established himself in the Saint-Merry district, and acted as godfather to the daughter of his friend Jean Patin and to the son of the Recorder of Poissy, all of which indicates that his father died at about this date. In 1544 we find him friendly with the painters Pallettre and Patin, and with Jean Hervé, "clerk to *M. le Général*" (presumably the *Receveur Général des Finances*). In 1547 he directed the arrangements for the funeral of Francis I. Guillaume Boutelou was working as one of his assistants. In 1548 he was friendly with Pierre Cuthe, and was said to be the father of two daughters, Catherine and Marguerite, although nothing is known of his wife. The years 1548–59 appear to have been fairly full; with the exception of the Uffizi *Henry II*, there are few portraits certainly by him from this period but a large number of chalk drawings. In 1559 he received seven ells of cloth on the occasion of the funeral of Henry II. He had made a death-mask of the King.

The years 1559–70 were probably the most crowded and brilliant of his career. Ronsard and Muret sang his praises, and in 1563 the Queen-Mother visited his studio.

After his death his offices passed not to his nephew Foulon, who was too young, but to Jean Decourt; part of the inheritance, including the portrait of Budé, the most famous production of the Clouet family, went to Jacques Patin.

François Clouet's art seems inferior to that of his father, to whom he remained faithful in every way. His portraits, which were so sought after in his own day, now seem a little sweet and lacking in force. This was no doubt in keeping with the taste of his sitters, none of whom seem to have sat to him after the age of forty. Undeterred, François Clouet continued until his death to produce portrait drawings in which the passage of time is indicated only by the change in costume. For his noble sitters, fashion was a matter of some importance; they made him write down what they were to be painted in, and many of his drawings are inscribed with notes such as "dress in tawny damask, striped Roanne velvet, white satin doublet". Sometimes they brought with them head-dresses, necklaces or diamonds, of which he made careful studies.

ÉTIENNE DELAUNE

about 1518–1583

Engraver, silversmith and medallist, born in Orleans, died probably in Strasbourg. In 1552 he was working at the Mint in Paris, and had a son, Louis, by Marie Robin; the birth certificate also states that his sister (?) Madeleine was married to Jean de France, *Valet de Chambre* to the King, and that Delaune was friendly with the great silversmith, Jehan Erondelle. In 1556 he was a master silversmith himself and had a daughter, Isabeau. In the same year he began to engrave allegories in honour of Henry II. He also engraved decorative subjects for silversmiths, based on the drawings of the Fontainebleau artists, Primaticcio, Niccolò dell'Abbate, Jean Cousin and Luca Penni. At the time of the Massacre of Saint Bartholomew, Delaune, a Protestant, was forced to leave Paris for Strasbourg. He went on to spend some years in Augsburg between 1576 and 1580. His last dated engraving (1582 not 1580) is a portrait of Ambroise Paré.

His son, Jean, born in 1559, made engravings after his father's works during the latter's last years (1579, 1580).

ÉTIENNE DU MOUSTIER

about 1520–1603

The most talented member of a dynasty of portrait painters and draughtsmen. Son of Geoffroy, brother of Pierre and Côme (the father of Pierre II and Daniel), he was born about 1520 and died in 1603 at the age of eighty-three.

Painter and *Valet de Chambre* to the King and the Queen-Mother, he probably worked under Clouet in the reign of Henry II, and held a more important position under his successors. His best period coincided with the reign of Henry III.

In his portraits he often used coloured chalks; they are more vigorous and incisive than those by Clouet.

JACQUES ANDROUET DU CERCEAU

about 1520–about 1585

Architect, decorator and engraver, born in 1520 (not 1510), died some time after 1584 in Switzerland where he had been obliged to take refuge on account of his religion.

In spite of Geymuller's researches, he remains a shadowy figure. He seems to have been a theorist and the head of a team of engravers rather than an architect proper. He was, however, held in great respect by both Charles IX and Renée de France, the Duchess of Ferrara.

His numerous theoretical works and his books on architecture and on optics, which are still almost unknown, have had less influence than his famous collection of drawings of *"les plus excellents bâtiments de France"*. This appeared in two volumes in 1576 and 1579 and illustrates, with no apparent plan, a number of sixteenth-century buildings with the accent on the years 1560 to 1575.

FRANÇOIS BUNEL THE YOUNGER

about 1550–about 1599

Born in Blois of a family of painters, son of François Bunel the Elder and grandson of Jean Bunel.

He was one of the first painters to go over to Henry IV and for a time, between 1583 and 1592, he was his only portraitist. As well as being a member of the Household, he followed the King on his campaigns. It was in this way that he drew the portrait of Henry IV at La Rochelle reproduced in this book.

JEAN COUSIN THE YOUNGER

about 1525–about 1594

Painter, born at Sens in about 1525 (rather than 1522), son of Jean Cousin the Elder, who wanted him to be a civil servant or an attorney and sent him to the Sorbonne in 1542. He decided, however, to follow his father's profession, probably as a result of a journey to Italy. He only emerges on the death of his father in 1563, when the town of Sens asked him to prepare a royal *Entry*, which never took place. In 1568 he drew a series of emblem drawings in his father's style for the engravers. He seems to have divided his time between Sens and Paris in the troubled years of Henry III's reign; at Sens he painted portraits and engraved an anatomical subject (an autopsy) in 1582. His reputation as a portraitist was considerable; he had several pupils and the Bibliothèque Nationale possesses a collection of chalk drawings done in his studio by one of his apprentices in 1578.

He was never as important as his father. The costume drawings which appeared in 1584 as "the work of Master Jean Cousin" were probably the work of Cousin the Elder, put to profit, as were many of the drawings, by his son. Unlike his father, he was never the foremost engraver of his time.

On the strength of an engraving by Pierre de Jode and a passage by Félibien, the *Last Judgment* in the Louvre is now reattributed to Cousin the Younger. It was painted for the Minimes of Vincennes, probably after the sack of 1589, and was formerly attributed to Cousin the Elder. This is borne out by the style of the picture, which is far removed from anything done in France between 1550 and 1560. Its Mannerist features, inspired by Italian engravings, date it nearer to the end of the century.

ANTOINE CARON

about 1527–about 1599

Painter, born in Beauvais, where he spent his early years working for stained-glass painters, notably Nicolas le Prince. He is said to have produced a *Last Judgment* and a *Life of Saint Genevieve* which have since disappeared.

He came to Paris some time before 1559, probably around 1555. He was friendly with Guyon Devable, another painter from Beauvais who kept up contacts with that town and sent there for an apprentice in 1559. Devable, who seems to have been a generation older than Caron, was also the brother-in-law of Nicolas Pinaigrier, the famous Beauvais stained-glass painter. In 1559 Caron joined Primaticcio and Niccolò dell'Abbate on the final stages of the decoration of the *Galerie d'Ulysse*. Starting low down in the scale at a salary of 14 *livres* per month, he quickly rose to a prominent position and in 1560 was entrusted with the "restoration" of numerous paintings, in particular those of the *Galerie François I.* His close collaboration with Niccolò dell'Abbate on the landscape decoration of the *Cabinet des Curiosités*, soon influenced his style and he turned to the painting of landscapes; he also loved to paint triumphal processions.

In 1561 Théodore de Bèze noted that the Court was impressed by two pictures representing the *Massacres of the Triumvirate* painted by Caron. The reasons for this success can be attributed as much to the painter's talent as to his choice of subject, which implied a comparison, to Protestants at least, between Roman and French methods of asserting sovereignty. One was immediately bought by the Protestants' defender, the Prince de Condé. These two pictures are only known to us indirectly, one in the form of a copy in the Museum at Beauvais, the other as an engraving on wood (reversed) by Jean de Gourmont.

In 1562 the apothecary Nicolas Houel honoured the Queen-Mother by commissioning from various French and Italian artists a series of drawings representing the story of Artemisia, celebrated, as was Catherine herself, for her love of her children. Caron seems to have supervised the work, aided by Niccolò dell'Abbate's assistants. For the same patron, and again with the Queen-Mother in view, Caron composed a "Pictorial History of France in our Time". In 1566 he painted yet another *Massacres of the Triumvirate* (Louvre), more elevated in style than his earlier compositions. Around the same time, 1566 or a little earlier, he painted *Augustus and the Sybil,* an allusion to the King's piety and fervent Catholicism.

In 1569 the City of Paris commissioned from him an *Entry of Charles IX into Paris.* Money was short at the time and the festivities never took place, but when the plan was mooted again in 1572, Niccolò, who had risen on the death of Primaticcio, was put in charge. In the preparations, Caron was assisted by a young Parisian painter of the Cousin circle called Jacques Couste, Courte or Comte. His name first appears in 1543; in 1559 he was in contact with Caron's rival Jacques Patin, and he was probably a pupil of Nicolas Halin who married Jehanne Cousin. Couste's son Nicolas became assistant to Jean Cousin the Younger.

In 1571 Caron painted *The Astronomers* (Coll. A. F. Blunt), a reference to the curious shower of red rain that fell on the 11th January after the uprooting of the Cross of the Gastines. This Cross had been planted by Catholics on the site of a destroyed Protestant house; its removal was supposed to be symbolical of the reconciliation between Catholics and Protestants so desired by the King. His counsellors interpreted the shower of blood as a sign of Heaven's displeasure at his policy of appeasement, and the Massacre of Saint Bartholomew took place the following year. On becoming Court Painter, Caron had found it expedient to go over to Rome. His position was further strengthened by the protection of the Queen-Mother, and the Court poets of the day claimed that he was superior to any Italian painter.

In 1572 he probably painted a series of the *Triumphs of the Seasons,* and in the same year prepared the festivities to celebrate the marriage of Marguerite de Valois and the King of Navarre, the future Henry IV. These, however, were interrupted by the Massacre of Saint Bartholomew. The following year he painted the *décor* for the *Entry into Paris of Henry III,* and acted as godfather to Antoine, son of the Nicolas Halin (or Hure) mentioned above.

He made his home in the rue Montorgueil, and as he was no longer receiving royal commissions, he prepared drawings for neighbouring wood-engravers, notably Alain de Mathonière. His daughters married the portraitist Pierre Gourdelle and two engravers who were to achieve fame, Thomas de Leu and Léonard Gaultier. It is likely that he collaborated with Gourdelle on portraits for rich patrons, and that he provided the two engravers with drawings of members of the Court.

In 1594 he painted an *Abraham and Melchisedec* (Coll. Ehrmann), an allegorical reference to Henry IV's entry into Paris. He went over to the new King and painted his portrait which was engraved by G. de Veen. His last work consisted of a series of drawings illustrating the *Icones* of Philostratus. The finished work appeared in 1614, but M. H.-J. Martin is right in saying that the drawings were finished and engraved by 1594.

Caron is one of the outstanding figures of the French Renaissance. Thomas de Leu's engraving shows him surrounded with the symbols not only of a painter but also of an architect or engineer and a writer or theorist, which indicates that there is still much to be learnt about him.

His friend Devable was in close contact with Claude Henriet (1550–1603). The latter was in Paris some time between 1574 and 1576, the time of Caron's greatest success, and was the master of Deruet, whose work shows traces of Caron's influence. This establishes a link between the Mannerism of Bellange and the graceful but limited art of Caron.

GEORGES REVERDY

Painter and engraver in a very individual style, born near Lyons, where he later worked. His name occurs in documents in 1529 and 1565.

JEAN DECOURT

about 1530–after 1585

Painter, born about 1530 in Limoges, where his contemporaries considered him to be a great and "estimable" man, the Apelles of his time. In his early years he worked for enamellers, and one of his enamels dated 1555, which represents Marguerite, the sister of Henry II, is in the Wallace Collection.

He went to Paris and made the portrait of an unknown man there in 1558. After the departure of Mary Stuart for Scotland in 1560, he received payments in 1562, 1567 and 1573 as her Painter, although he appears to have remained in Paris. This indicates that he worked for her when she was Queen of France in 1559.

We have no knowledge of his activity at the time when he must have been at the peak of his career. He next appears as painter to Henry II both before and after his accession. He succeeded Clouet without having anything like the same talent, but contemporaries seem to have admired him. He is known to have painted several portraits of Henry III, at least one of which was drawn after Clouet. Desportes wrote a poem on his portrait of

Mlle de Châteauneuf, Henry III's beautiful blonde mistress, and his friend the poet Joachim Blanchon entrusted him with the task of painting his lady:

> Peins moy, Decourt, sur le fondz d'un ovalle,
> L'ymage saint de ma belle Cipris.
> Si beau qu'il est, et qu'il y soit compris,
> La frise d'or qui sur ses flancs dévalle,
> Son teint rozin, qui à l'Aurore esgalle.
> Ses beaux yeux bruns qui sur tous ont le pris,
> De Mesme à ceux dont le Grec fust espris,
> Et ne la fais ou trop rouge ou trop palle.

He may have worked as a copyist in order to make a little money.

Decourt must not be confused with a painter known as "Court"; this could be a bad reading of "Couste", Caron's assistant.

He was succeeded by his son, Charles Decourt, in the reign of Henry IV.

MARC DUVAL

1530–1581

Painter, born at Saint-Vincent, on the outskirts of Le Mans. About 1550 he went to Italy to join the sculptor Ponce Jacquiau (not, as Vasari claims, an Italian whom he calls *Ponsio,* but nevertheless a member of the Accademia di San Lucca at Rome). Together they decorated the Palazzo Sacchetti (compare E. Hewett, *Gazette des Beaux-Arts,* 1928, vol. I, pp. 213–27). Duval, whom the Italians called "Marco Francese", worked for a time with Giulio Clovio, who was to be the master of El Greco. He returned to Paris about 1559–60 and received the title of "Painter to the Queen-Mother". He was famous for his miniatures and portraits and engraved decorative compositions from his own drawings.

In 1564–5, the Mannerist painter and engraver Bartholomew Spranger became an apprentice in his studio, after having worked in Antwerp with Floris. According to Van Mander, he spent "six weeks making copies of his master's drawings", then when he got bored with this, he covered the white walls of the *atelier* with vast compositions. Duval said, "My house is not large enough to contain this young man, he should be with a history painter", and took him to La Hamée (Van Mander, *Lives,* vol. I, p. 126, and *Gazette des Beaux-Arts,* 1868, vol. II, p. 35).

Duval lived in the rue de Grenelle (now rue Jean-Jacques Rousseau), next door to the Hôtel de la Ferrière, where Jeanne d'Albret was to die. This is an interesting coincidence and may go some way to explaining the painter's Protestant sympathies.

The son (not son-in-law) of Bertin Duval of Normandy, painter and sculptor to

Francis I (compare A.A.F., 1862, pp. 34–6), Marc married Catherine le Jolly or le Jolis, and had one daughter, Elizabeth, about 1570, and three sons (1577–9).

La Croix du Maine, who mentions him "because he came from the Maine region and admired anyone else who did", tells us that he was painter to Charles IX, who nicknamed him Duval the Deaf "because he was hard of hearing". He adds that Duval had "taken the likeness of many kings, queens, princes, princesses and nobles of France, which he himself engraved". The engravings, which have disappeared, were probably unfinished when he died on the 13th September, 1581, a date which he appears to have foreseen. His wife died in 1587 at their house in the rue de Grenelle.

Their daughter Elizabeth, who, according to La Croix du Maine, was "excellent with her pencil", is known to us only by an anonymous portrait of her rather unlovely features, done about 1595.

Duval's only documented work is the portrait of the Coligny brothers (plate 87), but Dimier (compare *Bulletin de la Société Nationale des Antiquaires de France*, 1933, pp. 81–2, with plates), working on the basis of a portrait of Sebastien de Luxembourg-Martigues, has found several works which could be attributed to him.

BENJAMIN FOULON

about 1533–about 1600

Painter, son of Abel Foulon, a brilliant mathematician who was popular at Court, and of Catherine, sister of François Clouet. His father, although born at Loue in the Maine region in 1513, came originally from an Antwerp family.

Very little is known of Foulon. Unlike most of the artists of his day, he seems to have been both rich and greedy. He made over-much of his connection with Clouet, and in spite of a very skimpy and conventional style, he obtained Clouet's property after his death.

On the basis of a portrait drawing of the Duc de Vendôme about 1596, signed *Fulonius fecit*, Dimier attributes to him some forty works done in "a lifeless and stodgy manner". Foulon became painter to Henry III shortly before the latter's death, and he retained the office under Henry IV, for whom he painted battle scenes in 1592.

ÉTIENNE DUPÉRAC

about 1535–1604

Architect, painter and engraver, born in Bordeaux. Much work remains to be done on this important artist. He spent some years in Italy from about 1554 to 1580. In Rome he engraved the *Festa di Testaccio*, a collection of *Antichità* (1575), and Michelangelo's *Last Judgment* as well as Roman *festas*, and was employed as an architect by the Conclave in 1572. He then went on to Venice where he made several sets of engravings after landscape drawings of the Titian School. On his return to France he became architect to Charles de Lorraine; in 1582, according to Mollet, the Duc d'Aumale entrusted him with the upkeep of his gardens, especially that of Anet; in 1578, as Stephanot du Pérac, he inspected the state of the walls of Caen (*Soc. Savantes dép.*, vol. XXI, p. 125). Round about this time he painted ruins and landscapes with the story of Callisto in the *Appartement des Bains* at Fontainebleau.

He then worked for Henry IV, was probably the architect of the Château Neuf of Saint-Germain-en-Laye and was almost certainly responsible for the idea of its Italian-style, terraced gardens. He held an important position at Court, making designs for various projects (among them a tomb, as M. P. Marot has shown), and advising on many different matters. Had he not died when he did, he might have held a position comparable to that of Primaticcio or of Mansart.

GERMAIN PILON
1537–1590

Born in Paris, the son of André Pilon, a sculptor from Le Mans who had settled there. Germain was a pupil of his father, who was well thought of, then worked with his two future brothers-in-law, the sculptor Michel Gaultier and the painter and engraver Nicolas Leblond. As Professor Blunt has pointed out, he formed his first manner on the stucco work of Primaticcio, the engravings of Domenico del Barbiere and the sculptured reliefs of Pierre Bontemps.

His name appears in the Royal Accounts in 1558. His most important works are the monument for the heart of Henry II (1560–3), the tomb of Henry II and Catherine de' Medici (1563–70), the monument of Chancellor de Birague and the tomb of his wife, Valentine Balbiani. He also sculpted numerous portrait busts and medallions, bas-reliefs, and a large scheme of decoration for the Valois Chapel at Saint-Denis (about 1583), part of which is preserved in the Church of Saint-Jean-Saint-François. His tombs were taken as models of their kind for many years.

He had many assistants including his sons, and Barthélémy Prieur continued his traditions.

The little-known inventory of Pilon's belongings, published by Coyecque in 1940, shows that the following objects were found in his possession after his death: forty of his own drawings, "a roll of sketches and scribbles", several rolls of architectural drawings, "a sketch of Notre Dame", drawings for other statues, and "nine boxes of portraits of Kings", no doubt portrait drawings by Clouet which had been lent to him to help in the execution of busts and medallions.

AMBROISE DUBOIS

1542/43–1614

This painter, who was immediately rechristened Dubois in France by the French, was in fact a native of Antwerp called Bosschaert. He came to France at an early date, probably around 1560, but no mention is made of his work before 1600, when he was employed by Henry IV at Fontainebleau (*Galerie de Diane, Chambre Ovale, Cabinet de Clorinde*).

The choice of this rather hackneyed exponent of international Mannerism at the age of more than sixty can probably be explained by the fact that in or around 1595 he married Françoise d'Hoey, daughter of the Curator of Pictures at Fontainebleau and sister-in-law of Fréminet.

It seems likely, therefore, that Dubois came to Fontainebleau rather earlier than is generally accepted, probably after the terrible siege of Antwerp of 1585, and that, like Fréminet, he was employed by d'Hoey on restorations and in this capacity presented to the King. In accordance with the custom of the day, d'Hoey rewarded his assistants by giving them his daughters in marriage.

Dubois, possibly related to a certain Claude Dubois who is mentioned as a sculptor and painter in Paris from 1571 onwards, married a second time and in 1604 had a son, Jean, who like d'Hoey became Curator of Pictures at Fontainebleau. He in his turn married the daughter of the King's *Valet de Chambre*, Antoine Oultrebon (whom his father had known in 1602), and had a son to whom he passed on the appointment in 1674.

MASTER OF THE MONOGRAM I.D.C.

about 1545/50–1600

Painter, about whom nothing is known, who signed a drawing of a Parisian *bourgeoise* (now in the Bibliothèque Nationale) with the initials I.D.C. (about 1580). He was discovered by Henri Bouchot, the first to appreciate his work, which consists of some twenty drawings (Dimier reduces the number to sixteen). These include a portrait of Gabrielle d'Estrées (plate 93), one of Mme de Carnavalet, and several portraits of unknown sitters covering the years 1573 to 1600.

HENRI LERAMBERT

about 1550–about 1610

Parisian painter, mentioned as "Master Painter" in 1580 and in 1600 as *Peintre ordinaire du Roi* (presumably Henry III as he does not appear in the Accounts of Henry IV). He came from a family of sculptors, all of whom had worked at Fontainebleau since 1537 at the latest; the youngest being apprenticed to their elders. The last-known member of the dynasty was Louis Lerambert (1614–90). He worked as a sculptor at Versailles and was a pupil of Vouet and Sarrazin, godchild of Louis XIII and member of the *Académie Royale*.

The Cabinet des Estampes of the Bibliothèque Nationale possesses a number of drawings of different periods catalogued under his name, presumably because they came from his *atelier*.

JEAN BOUCHER

1563–1633

Painter and engraver, born in Bourges in 1563, died in 1633. No work has been done on him apart from an article published in 1845 by H. Boyer, with later additions by the Comte de Chennevières.

Jean Boucher was the son of Pierre Boucher, a modest painter of Bourges. He seems to have stayed in his native town where he rose to a certain eminence in 1598 on the occasion of the preparations for the *Entry of Henry IV*, which eventually did not take place.

In 1600 he was in Rome and it was there that he made the drawing reproduced in plate 96. He made further journeys to Rome in 1621 and 1625.

In Bourges he had an *atelier* of some importance, and one of his apprentices, taken on in 1621 when he needed extra help for the *Entry of Louis XIII*, was the young Pierre Mignard, aged twelve.

He was looked upon favourably by the Chapter of Notre-Dame-de-Bourges who seem to have arranged an *atelier* for him in one of the towers of the church. In his will he left considerable sums to the Convent of his native town, and to four of his pupils he left "all my drawings and engravings" to be divided amongst them.

MARTIN FRÉMINET

1567–1619

Painter, born in Paris in 1567, died in 1619. Son of the painter Médéric Fréminet and father of Louis, who was also an artist.

We know nothing of his early years, which is not surprising as they were overshadowed by the wars of the Catholic League, which left little time for patronage. It was probably for this reason that he left for Italy in 1592. His biographers tell us that he was friendly with the Cavaliere d'Arpino and that he studied the works of Michelangelo and Parmigianino. He returned to France via Savoy, where he worked for a time.

On his arrival in Paris at the end of the century, he attracted the attention of Henry IV who made him his Court Painter and *Valet de Chambre*. Fréminet became one of the most important artists of what is known as the Second School of Fontainebleau.

LAGNEAU

Draughtsman and possibly painter of the last years of the sixteenth century known to us only by his pseudonym of Lagneau. He is characterized by a love of strong expressions. Although there has been a tendency to minimize the importance of this trend, it reveals Lagneau not only as a man of his time, which, according to Laborde, was "cynical in the extreme", but also as the forerunner of later caricaturists and modern expressionists.

NOTES ON THE PLATES

See table of abbreviations, page 138

JEAN FOUQUET
about 1415–about 1480

2

Guillaume Juvénal des Ursins. Before 1460. Black and coloured chalks. 026×019. Berlin, Print Room.

Study for the portrait of the Chancellor now in the Louvre. One of the earliest examples of the use of coloured chalk.

Hist.: Coll. Rumohr, sold Dresden, 1846, no. 3388a; Berlin, Print Room; Exh. *French Art*, London, R.A., 1932, no. 620; Exh. *Chefs-d'œuvre*, Paris, 1937, no. 438.
Bibl.: M. J. Friedländer, "Eine Bildnisstudie Jean Fouquets", in *Berlin Jahrbuch*, 1910, p. 227; G. Ring, p. 212, no. 127; Ch. Stierling, *Les Primitifs*, p. 74.

FRENCH SCHOOL
Fifteenth century

3

Study of a woman kneeling. Pen-and-ink. 035×025. Paris, École des Beaux-Arts.

Discovered by Pierre Lavallée, who emphasized the beauty and simplicity of this drawing, which he thought might have been prepared for an engraving. Although done on paper with a watermark of the Loire region, he attributed it to the School of Moulins.

FRENCH SCHOOL
Late fifteenth century

4

"*King René.*" About 1476. Coloured chalk. 033×024. Sixteenth-century inscription. Bibliothèque Nationale, Cabinet des Estampes, Na. 21 rés., p. 30.

Like the Louvre portraits, based on the portrait of King René by Nicolas Froment in the *Altarpiece of the Burning Bush* at Aix-en-Provence. In about 1476 the King had copies made for members of his Court. He was fond of "portraits in lead", and in the Inventory of his collection, Lecoy de la Marche mentions a "drawing in lead" on a dresser in his room "representing the late Duke of Milan" as well as several "portraits drawn in lead" of himself, his wife and several nobles in a sort of wooden frame. He also kept in the handle of his lance a roll of parchment "where could be seen the portrait of the Queen", his wife.

The King was then sixty-seven and had five more years to live. He is wearing one of those fur-lined black hats described in his Inventories, and his rather puffy eyes bear witness to the constant use of the spectacles which we know he wore in 1476.

Hist.: From an album in the early B.N. collection. A typical contemporary copy.

FRENCH SCHOOL
about 1500

5

Portrait of a young girl. Black chalk. 015×010. Louvre, Cabinet des Dessins.

Bouchot attributes this very fine drawing to the Master of Moulins.

Bibl.: Cat. of the Exh., *Les Primitifs Français*, 1904, no. 363.

LEONARDO DA VINCI
1452–1519

6

Standing figure: study of drapery. About 1518. Black chalk on white paper. 021×013. Windsor, Royal Collection.

One of the last drawings (Popp says definitely the last) made by Leonardo in France. Possibly a study for a masquerade commanded by King Francis I.

Hist.: Coll. Leonardo; Coll. Melzi; Coll. P. Leoni. *Bibl.:* K. Clark, *Leonardo drawings . . . Windsor*, no. 12581.

SCHOOL OF LEONARDO
about 1518

7

View of Amboise, seen from below. Red chalk on white paper. 013×026. Windsor, Royal Collection.

From the album of Leonardo drawings now at Windsor, originally the property of Melzi who left France with them immediately after Leonardo's death in 1519.

Sir Kenneth Clark, who has made a study of the drawing, does not consider it to be by Leonardo, but probably by Andrea Solario, who, as it happens, was at the French Court in 1518.

The drawing was almost certainly used by Leonardo in his studies for the layout of the gardens at Blois, on which there are notes in the *Codex Atlanticus.*

Hist.: Coll. Leonardo; Coll. Melzi; Coll. P. Leoni. *Bibl.:* K. Clark, *op. cit.*, no. 12727.

LEONARDO DA VINCI
1452–1519

8

Idea for the Château of Romorantin. 1518. Black chalk on white (French) paper. 024×018. Windsor, Royal Collection.

M. Heydenreich identified this drawing as a project for the elevation of Romorantin. It is extremely significant as it anticipates Chambord and shows that Leonardo was in part responsible for the style of architecture of the Loire châteaux.

The Château of Romorantin was destined for the Queen-Mother, Louise of Savoy; the King also intended to make use of it from time to time. He had been thinking about it since 1515, and there is in existence a letter from his mother, unfortunately not dated, telling him that she has been to Blois "and have inspected the work in progress, not before time. From Blois I am come (to Romorantin) for the same purpose."

Now in a note Leonardo says, "The day before the feast of St Anthony, I went from Romorantin to Amboise, and the King left Romorantin two days earlier." The feast of St Anthony falls on the 17th January. The 16th January in question cannot refer to 1517, for Leonardo had not yet arrived in France, but is probably 1518, when we know the King to have been at Amboise (cf. his Itinerary in vol. VIII of *Actes du Roi*, 1905).

The château, which Leonardo has drawn on the back of a study for a leg of the horse in the Trivulzio monument, consists of a square building fortified with towers, containing four *appartements* and a fine façade with a staircase leading to a canal which could be used for water parties. Octagonal wooden structures would have been set up round a courtyard to house important visitors (an idea which was later developed in the *pavillons* of Marly).

The foundations were laid; the elevation rose to a height of ten feet, and the labourers were still being paid in 1525 (*Actes du Roi*, vol. VI, p. 462). But the building yards were ravaged by an epidemic and Romorantin was abandoned for Chambord, which began to rise in 1524 (Pontbriant having been made overseer the 6th September, 1519).

Hist.: From the same album as plates 6 and 7. *Bibl.:* L. H. Heydenreich, "Leonardo da Vinci, architect to Francis I", in *Burl. Mag.*, 1952, pp. 277–85; K. Clark, *op. cit.*, no. 12292 v.

STUDIO OF LEONARDO
about 1517–20

9

Nude Study of the Gioconda. Black chalk, wash. 330×230. Chantilly, Musée Condé.

M. de Hevesy has made a study of these nude Giocondas (usually attributed to Leonardo's pupils) of which a number could be found in France in the 1520's. It is possible that one of them was the "Florentine lady done from nature" ("*Dona fiorentina, facta di naturale*") which the Cardinal of Aragon saw at Cloux in 1517. This suggestion, which has been put forward before, is based on a translation of the Italian text different from the one that is usually given, and also on the fact that the drawing was done for that notorious libertine Giuliano de' Medici. The latter died in 1516, which explains why Leonardo still had the drawing in 1517.

Clouet's half-length portraits of women bathing derive from this type of nude Gioconda, which also inspired a certain number of poems, notably Clément Marot's *Éloge du Beau Têtin* (1534):

> Têtin de satin blanc tout neuf,
> Têtin qui fait honte à la rose . . .

In another poem, Marot rails against those "who have followed his epistle to a beautiful breast with others" (to their lady's hair, heart, thigh, hand, eye, ear, eyebrow, etc.).

Bibl: De Hevesy, "Les Jocondes Nues", in *Gazette des Beaux-Arts*, 1931, vol. I, pp. 114 and 119; cf. also *G.B.A.*, 1880, vol. II, p. 379.

UNKNOWN ARTIST
about 1515

10

Battle of Marignano, 1515. Pen-and-ink with touches of colour. 021×031. Chantilly, Musée Condé.

This frightful battle, which Marshal Trivulzio called "a conflict of giants", took place on the 13th and 14th September, 1515. The Swiss (on the left) would have won had they not been attacked from the rear by the Venetians. In the foreground is Francis I surrounded by his knights, and on the left a nude figure, no doubt the Comte de Guise who was found buried under a pile of corpses and who took three months to recover from the shock.

Lemonnier, who was the first to discover the drawing (but not to reproduce it), attributed it to the Master with the Rat-trap, Nat. Dati, who engraved a scene of the Battle of Fornovo (Bartsch, vol. XIII, pp. 364–66). It could equally well be by an Italian working at the French Court.

Bibl.: Lemonnier in *B.A.F.*, 1923, vol. I, pp. 7–8.

JEAN CLOUET
about 1475/80–about 1541

11

Odet de Foix, Seigneur de Lautrec. About 1515. Black and red chalk with traces of water-colour at the bottom. 033×023. Chantilly, Musée Condé.

Brother of the King's mistress, Mme de Châteaubriand, and one of the finest of French captains. Famous for his campaigns in Italy, he was made a Marshal of France in 1515, and was the French governor in Milan until defeated in the Battle of Bicocca.

He was disgraced by the King, then recalled and made Lieutenant-General in command of the forces of the Holy League. He died in the Siege of Naples of 1528.

This portrait has been wrongly inscribed, and called Th. de Foix, "sieur de Lescun", Odet's younger brother, whose capitulation at Cremona led to the final defeat of the French in Italy.

Bibl.: Chantilly, 55; M.N., 136; D., 1.

12

"Mgr d'Angousme, son of Francis I." About 1524–27. Black chalk, worked up in the face and left hand. Bottom right, smudge of red chalk and traces of black. 033×023. Chantilly, Musée Condé.

Charles de France, Duc d'Angoulême, son of Francis I, was born in 1523 and died in 1545. Clouet also portrayed his elder brother François, who died at an equally early age (drawing at Chantilly, painting at Antwerp).

Hist.: Coll. Catherine de' Medici; Medici family until eighteenth century; Lenoir; Gower; Duc d'Aumale.
Bibl.: Chantilly, 67; M.N., 8; D., 46.

13

"The Bailiff of Caen." About 1530. Red and black chalk. 033×023. Chantilly, Musée Condé.

Aymée Motier de la Fayette, governess to Jeanne d'Albret and *baillive* of the town of Caen, married Louis XII's outspoken Equerry, François de Silly, who became governor of Chantilly and was killed at Pavia in 1525. She was directly responsible for the death of Henry IV's elder brother, Henri, Duc de Beaumont. He was given into her care as a new-born baby, but "being old and shivery and living as she did on top of the fire in a hermetically sealed room, she made him pant and sweat with the heat", so much so "that he slowly suffocated in his wrappings" while she repeated, "Leave him alone, he's better off sweating than freezing to death."

Hist.: Coll. Catherine de' Medici; Medici family until the eighteenth century; Lenoir; Gower; Duc d'Aumale.
Bibl.: Chantilly, 112; M.N., 198; D., 19.

14

Guillaume Budé. About 1535. Black chalk with dark smudge in the centre. 033×023. Chantilly, Musée Condé.

Budé (1467–1540) is shown at the age of seventy. He himself noted that his portrait was being drawn by Clouet, *pictor iconicus*. This is confirmed by Thevet, who reproduces the work in his *Hommes Illustres*. Budé, an outstanding Greek and Latin scholar, was the father of the Collège de France. Erasmus called him "the Wonder of France". The original drawing remained the property of Clouet; a painting, referred to as "*figure de M. Budé*", is mentioned in the inventory of Jacques Patin (sixteenth century), while another belonged to Budé's heirs. Mr Popham has published a painting (*Burl. Mag.*, March 1923), which bears the erroneous name of Finé. This has a background of the same grey as the smudge on our drawing, which proves that the latter was used as a preliminary study for the portrait.

Hist.: See above.
Bibl.: Chantilly, 143; M.N., 132; D., 88.

15

Leonora de Sapata. About 1530. Black and red chalk. 033×023. Chantilly, Musée Condé.

Lady-in-waiting to Queen Eleanor of Portugal, whom she accompanied from Spain to Paris on the occasion of her marriage to Francis I in 1530. She was sent back to Spain in 1537. The Queen, who was ignored by her husband, took it out on her ladies-in-waiting in a somewhat startling fashion. Dr Parker has found the following note in a collection of sixteenth-century drawings, which belonged in the seventeenth century to François Brisacier and are now in the Ashmolean Museum (*Cat.*, vol. I, p. 171): "She took great pleasure in having her ladies-in-waiting undress and whip each other, all making different movements of their buttocks. The better they were at this, the more she enjoyed it."

Bibl.: Chantilly, 98; M.N., 172; D., 75.

FRENCH SCHOOL
about 1526

16

"*The late Queen of Navarre, Marguerite.*" Black chalk with white highlights. 033×023. Chantilly, Musée Condé.

Dimier attributed this drawing to "the fourth imitator of the so-called Jean Clouet". In other words, it is by a Court painter contemporary with Clouet but less talented than him.

The portrait gains an additional lustre from the personality of the sitter, Marguerite, sister of Francis I, patroness of poets and of the earliest Huguenots. She is shown here as a widow, which indicates that she is in mourning for the Duc d'Alençon (died in 1525) and has not yet married Henri d'Albret (1527).

Bibl.: Chantilly, 42; M.N., 43; D., 205.

ROSSO
1495–1540

17

La Vierge de la Miséricorde. End of 1529. Red chalk. 029×026. Louvre, Cabinet des Dessins.

Study for the decoration of the Capella della Fraternità at Arezzo. One of the drawings which Rosso brought from Italy and which was used as a model by his earliest French pupils. Proof of this can be found in the numerous copies in existence (at least two in the Louvre).

Hist.: Louvre, 1579.
Bibl.: Paola Barocchi, *Il Rosso Fiorentino*, pp. 73–74; Kusenberg, *Rosso*, no. 70.

18

An Incantation. About 1532–35. Pen-and-wash. 043 ×029. Paris, École des Beaux-Arts.

Signora Barocchi has made a careful study of this drawing, which she considers to be the most significant of Rosso's French period. She has emphasized the dramatic atmosphere of the scene: the long-haired old woman, the two strange beauties, the gestures of their long hands, the ruin, the hanging foliage, the mask-like faces. A drawing of such quality is rare in Rosso's *œuvre.*

Hist.: Coll. J. Masson, exh. 1921, no. 47, as by René Boyvin; given by him to the École des Beaux-Arts, no. 1194.
Bibl.: Kusenberg, "An Incantation Scene", in *O.M.D.*, 1929, p. 62; P. Barocchi, *op. cit.*, p. 215.

19

Vertumnus and Pomona. About 1532–35. Pen-and-wash, partly squared for transfer. 027×016. Louvre, Cabinet des Dessins.

In an orchard surrounded by a fence in order to keep out suitors, the nymph Pomona receives the young Vertumnus. As Ovid tells us (*Met.* XIV, 654ff.), he has disguised himself as an old messenger woman, has covered his head with a turban and a few white hairs, and leans on a crutch. He is enumerating on his fingers reasons why she should help him. She listens with a smile, for she has already seen him as a harvester, a haymaker, a shepherd, a tree-lopper, a fruit-picker, a soldier and a fisherman. "By dint of many disguises, he found many opportunities to approach his love" (*Met.*, XIV, 653), who soon relented.

PRIMATICCIO
about 1504–70

20

Venus and Cupid. About 1539–40. Red chalk, squared. 027×016. Louvre, Cabinet des Dessins.

Belongs to a series of ten studies for spandrels of the arcades of the lower gallery or *Salle du Conseil* at Fontainebleau. This gallery, facing on to the lake, runs from the King's Apartment to the Chapel. The ten compositions were engraved by the L.D. Master about 1545.

Hist.: Louvre, inv. 8557.
Bibl.: Dimier, 44.

21

A Naiad. About 1552–56. Red chalk with white. 159×210. Louvre, Cabinet des Dessins.

Study for the first picture of the seventh window of the Ballroom at Fontainebleau. Pendant to an *Amphion.*

Hist.: Des Nœuds de la Noue; Royal Coll. in the seventeenth century (*paraphe* of Coypel and de Cotte).
Bibl.: *Cat.*, 8542; Dimier, 29.

22

Study of a gisant. About 1550. Red chalk with white. 023×012. Louvre, Cabinet des Dessins.

One of the first drawings after a nude model to be done in France; almost certainly for the tomb in the following plate.

Hist.: Royal Coll., inv. 8612.
Bibl.: Dimier, drawings 65.

23

Project for a tomb. 1550. Pen-and-bistre. 042×032. Louvre, Cabinet des Dessins.

As Dimier has pointed out, this is a drawing not for the tomb of Henry II, but for that of Claude de Lorraine, ancestor of the Guise family, who died in 1550, and of his wife Antoinette de Bourbon. There is a study of caryatids, also for this tomb, in the Louvre (inv. 8580; Dimier, 67).

This composition shows an attempt to combine the naturalism of the *gisants*, seen at a more highly developed stage in the tomb of Henry II, with the statues of Virtues which had been so popular with an earlier generation.

A drawing in the Clairambault Collection shows that the design was executed, though with marked differences, by Domenico Fiorentino and Leroux, called Picard (the first payments were made to them about 1551).

Hist.: Royal Coll., inv. 8579.
Bibl.: Dimier, drawings no. 66 and pp. 334–41.

24

Bacchus. Red chalk with white. 026×014. Louvre, Cabinet des Dessins.

Hist.: Inv. 8596.
Bibl.: Dimier, 83.

25

Two old men seated. About 1552–56. Red chalk with white. 017×020. Louvre, Cabinet des Dessins.

Studies for one of the windows of the Ballroom at Fontainebleau. Sculptors made use of them for the semi-reclining figures which they placed on tombs.

Hist.: Royal Coll., inv. 8546.
Bibl.: Dimier, drawings 33.

26

The Rape of Europa. About 1541–44. Pen-and-ink. 023×021. Louvre, Cabinet des Dessins.

One of Primaticcio's earliest works. This drawing, which does not appear to have been used for a painting, was engraved by the L.D. Master.

Hist.: Coll. Mariette, who, when discussing the engraving in the *Abecedario,* says, "I have the original drawing."
Bibl.: R.F. 567 (1870); printed cat., no. 91; Dimier, drawings 120.

27

Nymph and Cupid. Red chalk with white. 021×029. Louvre, Cabinet des Dessins.

Hist.: Coll. Mariette.
Bibl.: Cat. ms., no. 8522; printed cat., no. 272.

28

Diana bathing with her Nymphs. About 1541–47. Pen-and-ink with bistre and some white, squared. 214 ×346. Louvre, Cabinet des Dessins.

The left half of a drawing, the other half of which shows a river and dogs (British Museum). This composition, which inspired twenty other drawings, paintings and engravings, shows the discovery by Diana that Callisto is pregnant by Jupiter. It was worked up into a lunette-shaped painting on the ceiling of the *Appartement des Bains* at Fontainebleau, and is no doubt the picture that Cassiano del Pozzo refers to in his description of the apartments as "the bath and the pregnancy" ("*il bagno e la gravidanza*").

Hist.: Royal Coll., inv. 8521.
Bibl.: Dimier, 163.

29

Ceres. About 1560–70. Red chalk with white. 023 ×022. Louvre, Cabinet des Dessins.

This fine drawing was recently attributed to Primaticcio, although it seems more likely to have been the work of a sculptor. Goujon left behind him a taste for figures of this type to be used on the façades of royal palaces.

Hist.: Inv. 8770.

30

Study of a nude woman carrying fruit in a drapery. Black chalk, drawn over again, squared. 026×011. Louvre, Cabinet des Dessins.

According to Reiset, "a doubtful attribution". One of the first academies drawn in France; the woman's artificially contrived pose shows that the right hand of the model was supported on a high crutch. A very fine early Mannerist drawing, close in style to the *Rape of Helen,* which, as Mme Béguin has shown, was used as a study for the picture in the Bowes Museum.

Hist.: Royal Coll. (*paraphe* of Coypel); Inv. 8532.
Bibl.: Dimier, 419, wrongly attributed.

SCHOOL OF PRIMATICCIO

31

Diana and Actaeon. 1560–70. Pen-and-wash, with white. 023×028. Louvre, Cabinet des Dessins.

Diana throws water over the intruder who begins to turn into a stag. This theme was very popular with the Fontainebleau School.

Hist.: R.F., 564.
Bibl.: Dimier, 119, 90.

STUDIO OF PRIMATICCIO

32

Portrait of the artist as an old man. Red chalk. 016 ×012. Vienna, Albertina.

This portrait shows Primaticcio, the real creator of the Renaissance style in France, at the end of his life, about 1560–70, when he felt exhausted and outstripped by younger artists. Compare the portrait of François Clouet, plate 59.

Hist.: Coll. Mariette; Coll. Lagoy.
Bibl.: Dimier, 143; A. Stix and A. Spitzmuller, *Albertina Cat.*, vol. IV, no. 32; Inv., 1965; Cat. of *Albertina Exhibition*, Paris, 1952, no. 129.

PRIMATICCIO

33

Sheep-shearing. About 1560–70. Pen with some body-colour. 031×021. Louvre, Cabinet des Dessins.

Symbol of the month of June. There is a similar drawing in the Louvre. Very near in feeling to the Bassani.

Hist.: Former Royal Coll. (*paraphe* of Coypel and Robert de Cotte); Inv. 8639.

34

Study for one of the stucchi for the room of the Duchesse d'Étampes at Fontainebleau. About 1541–44. Pen-and-wash. 0,250×0,170. Louvre, Cabinet des Dessins.

The drawing is more successful than the finished work, where the women, no longer nude, support the frame. One of Primaticcio's earliest works after his return from Rome, where he had been sent by Francis I. Payments were made to Pierre Patin and Guidon Le Doux for the paintings in this room about 1541. The composition was engraved in 1544 (Herbet, 257).

Hist.: Coll. His de la Salle.

STUDIO OF PRIMATICCIO

35

Rebecca giving Eliezer to drink. About 1550. On reddish paper with white highlights. 266×328. Louvre, Cabinet des Dessins.

This drawing and its pendant, *Esau blessing Jacob*, were formerly in the collection of Crozat. Mariette considered them to be drawn after paintings by Primaticcio "probably by Luca Penni or one of his other pupils. . . . They are of great importance, for in addition to being beautifully drawn, they were never engraved." Dimier gives them to Primaticcio. It seems probable that the two drawings were made for a patron who sent them back because they were overcrowded.

Hist.: Coll. Crozat.
Bibl.: Inv. 8511; Cat. Morel d'Arleux, no. 4629; Dimier, 3.

36

The Diana of Anet. About 1550. Black chalk. 025 ×018.

Du Colombier interprets this most convincingly as "the idea of a painter destined to be carried out in sculpture". The artist is certainly from the immediate circle of Primaticcio to whom the drawing has long been attributed. A. F. Blunt gives the finished statue in the Louvre not to Goujon but to the young Germain Pilon. The statue, which was executed about 1550, is certainly based on this drawing and could be the immature work of a young sculptor following another's design.

Hist.: Inv. 26720.
Bibl.: Du Colombier, *Jean Goujon*, pp. 131–33; A. F. Blunt, *Art and Architecture in France, 1500–1700*, p. 86, notes 122–24.

FRENCH SCHOOL

about 1550 or a little earlier

37

"Triboulet", the King's Fool. Red chalk. 033 × 023. Chantilly, Musée Condé.

This witty and agreeable fool was probably the second of his name. M. Charles Terrasse quotes Jean Marot's description of him:

> "Petit front et grands yeux, nez grand, taillé à vote,
> Estomach plat et long, haut dos à porter hotte."

In *Le Roi s'Amuse* (1832), Victor Hugo gives him a very different character: "Triboulet is deformed, Triboulet is ill, Triboulet is court jester, and these three misfortunes have soured his nature."

Bibl.: Chantilly, 103; M.N., 180; D., 337.

FRENCH SCHOOL

about 1540–45

38

Henry II as a young man. Black chalk. 033 × 022. Chantilly, Musée Condé.

Described at this period with some insight by Venetian ambassadors as "of a rather melancholy disposition . . . excellent at feats of arms . . . not over-intelligent".

Bibl.: M.N., 13.

GEORGES REVERDY

39

Adoration of the Shepherds. About 1550–60. Pen and bistre wash with body-colour on toned paper. 140 × 270. Paris, École des Beaux-Arts.

Almost certainly by Reverdy, the most talented painter of the Lyons School, and almost the only French artist of his time to show an interest in *effets de nuit.*

Hist.: Masson Gift, no. 1177.

JEAN COUSIN

about 1525–about 1594

40

The Prophet Balaam and the Angel. About 1560. Pen-and-wash with some body-colour. 200 × 180. Rennes, Museum.

P. Lavallée attributes this drawing to Cousin the Younger, although it seems more likely to have been the work of his father.

Hist.: Coll. President de Robien.

Bibl.: P. Lavallée, *Musée de Rennes, 14 dessins,* 1939, p. 5.

SCHOOL OF FONTAINEBLEAU

41

Diana's Hunt. Pen-and-wash on toned paper. 039 × 055. Rennes, Museum.

Tapestry cartoon for a series representing the story of Diana, of which two other episodes are extant.

Hist.: Coll. Robien.

Bibl.: P. Lavallée, *Musée de Rennes, 14 dessins,* 1939, no. 2.

STYLE OF JEAN COUSIN

42

Bacchic scene. About 1550. Vienna, Albertina.

This drawing, reproduced by kind permission of Herr Hofmann, who is making a study of it, is certainly close in style to Cousin's engravings.

SCHOOL OF JEAN COUSIN

43

Jupiter and a Nymph. Pen-and-ink. 033 × 017. Bibliothèque Nationale, Cabinet des Estampes, B 5 rés.

Hist.: Formerly in coll. of the Abbey of Sainte-Geneviève.

SCHOOL OF FONTAINEBLEAU

44

Justice. About 1560. Drawing heightened with body-colour. 180 × 140. Louvre, Cabinet des Dessins.

Decorative composition for a bowl or chalice in the style of Delaune but in a different technique.

Hist.: Royal Coll., inv. 8759.

ÉTIENNE DELAUNE
about 1520–1603

45

Children's games. About 1560. Pen-and-ink with bistre wash, on vellum. 110 × 170. Louvre, Cabinet des Dessins.

Rare example of a genre scene in the drawing of this period. Near in feeling to an interesting series of wood engravings by Guillaume le Bé: "36 subjects showing all the games ever invented and played by children . . ." (1587).

Hist.: Formerly coll. of His de la Salle, given to the Louvre in 1878.
Bibl.: Both de Tauzia, *Notices des Dessins H. de la S.*, no. 246; *Inventaire Guiffrey-Marcel*, no. 3548 (as *Une Crèche*).

46

Design for a ewer. Pen-and-wash on vellum. 024 × 010. Windsor, Royal Collection.

In the centre Apollo and Daphne. One of the many precious vases designed by sixteenth-century silversmiths which, owing to their value, are no longer in existence, having been melted down in periods of financial embarrassment.

Bibl.: A. F. Blunt, *French Drawings at Windsor Castle*, 1945, no. 5.

47

Music. About 1560. Pen-and-ink with slight bistre wash on vellum. 0,200 × 0,263. Louvre, Cabinet des Dessins.

Design for a tapestry belonging to a series in the style of the Fontainebleau School. Almost certainly by Delaune (cf. engravings, in particular his series of the Months). Miss Yates is preparing a study which will show the connections between this drawing and the circle of Nicolas Houel.

Hist.: Coll. His de la Salle, given to the Louvre in 1878.
Bibl.: *Inventaire Guiffrey-Marcel*, no. 3549.

JEAN DE GOURMONT THE ELDER
1483–1551

48

Massacre of the Innocents. Pen-and-wash. 021 × 032. Bibliothèque Nationale, Cabinet des Estampes, B 15 rés.

A typical work of the Lyons School, which specialized in the painting of ruins and architectural fragments. An eighteenth-century inscription, possibly by Mariette, attributes it to the painter and draughtsman Jacques Granthomme, whose style is, however, totally different.

FRENCH SCHOOL
about 1559

49

"Madame de Savoye when she was Madame Marguerite." Black and red chalk. 033 × 023. Chantilly, Musée Condé.

Daughter of Francis I. According to Ronsard, she took after her mother. She married the Duke of Savoy in 1559 at the age of thirty-five, after a prolonged engagement which was interrupted by wars. Her brother, Henry II, who loved her dearly, ceded to her the French possessions in Savoy, an unpopular action which (as Brantôme tells us) inspired the following remark: "She preserved her virginity for thirty-five years, then offered it up for the ruin of France." She died in 1574. Dimier attributes this portrait to the Master of Luxembourg-Martigues.

Bibl.: Chantilly, 278; M.N., 28; D., 566.

FRANÇOIS CLOUET
about 1516/20–72

50

"The great King Francis." 1547. Red chalk. 033×023. Chantilly, Musée Condé.

From the death-mask of the King made by Clouet, who hastened from Paris to Rambouillet to take an impress of the King's features in yellow wax. From this he made a plaster cast, then a wax cast on to which he stuck hair and beard (from a document discovered by Jal).

Shortly after the King's death, on the 6th April, 1547, Clouet engaged Marc Béchot, Jean Patin the Elder, Georges Le Doux, Jean Rondel, Gérard Josse and Pierre Prieur, to help him to prepare the funeral arrangements.

The death-mask was considered a great success. It was preserved by the Cardinal de Tournon (he had "the image of the body of Francis I which was carried at the King's funeral"); while Nicolas Houel had in his collection an "*Ecce Homo* four feet high containing a *gisant* of the late King Francis."

Bibl.: Chantilly 247; M.N., 4; D., 1320.

51

"La Duchesse de Valentinois." 1550. Black and red chalk. 033×023. Chantilly, Musée Condé.

Bibl.: Chantilly, 392; M.N., 202; D., 443.

52

"Charles IX." 1562. Black and red chalk. 330×230. Bibliothèque Nationale, Cabinet des Estampes, Na. 22.

The King "at the age of twelve". Many official portraits were painted from this drawing.

Bibl.: D., 454.

53

Marguerite de Valois "at the age of eight". 1559–60. Black chalk. 036×026. Bibliothèque Nationale, Cabinet des Estampes, Na. 21 rés., p. 63.

It appears that after the death of Henry II, Catherine de' Medici commissioned from Clouet portraits of herself and her children, of which this is one. The Princess who was to marry Henry IV and to become the most beautiful, the most elegant and the most captivating woman in France, is still a baby, but one can already see the luminous eyes of which Brantôme spoke, and the hair which darkened to black, but was always spoken of as fair.

The inscription at the bottom is in Catherine de' Medici's hand; the top one dates from the eighteenth century.

Bibl.: D., 716.

FRENCH SCHOOL
about 1550–59

54

Henry II on horseback. Black chalk. 035×025. Chantilly, Musée Condé.

Francis I was very anxious to leave an equestrian statue of himself but the sculptor Rustici died before finishing his "great bronze horse". Henry II had the same idea, and we know that a statue of him "on horseback, armed and victorious" was to be seen in 1559 in the courtyard of the Château of Oiron which belonged to his *Grand Ecuyer*. Moreover, in 1558, Jodelle had painted at the Hôtel de Ville a *Henry II on horseback* now known only by copies, but for which this is perhaps the original drawing. A miniature in the Musée Condé shows Henry II on horseback, but it is very different in style and probably executed as a pendant to one of Francis I. Finally, after the death of the King, Catherine de' Medici wanted an equestrian statue of him. Daniele da Volterra did not have time to complete the horse, of which a cast ("the white horse") was sent to Fontainebleau, before he himself died. The statue was never executed. Ronsard, who had been the King's page, wrote of his passion for horses, and his grace when he was mounted:

> "Quant à bien manier et piquer un cheval
> La France n'eut jamais ni n'aura son égal.
> Et semble que son corps naisse hors de la selle
> Centaure ni cheval . . ."
>
> (*Hymne de Henri II . . .* 1555)

Hist.: Coll. Catherine de' Medici.
Bibl.: Chantilly, 334; D., 1307.

FRANÇOIS CLOUET

55

Catherine de' Medici. 1560–70 (?). Black chalk. 033×022. Bibliothèque Nationale, Cabinet des Estampes, Na. 22.

This portrait is difficult to date in view of the fact that the Queen-Mother, who was unhealthy, "pale and sallow" in her youth, took on new life in her old age. As late as 1577, Lippomano tells us, she was extremely well-preserved: "she has scarcely a wrinkle on her face, which is round and full; her lower lip is strongly marked like that of all her children. She still wears mourning, with a black veil falling to her shoulders but leaving her face uncovered." She had lost her hair at an early date and in the Royal Accounts for 1558 mention is made of 5 sous given "to a poor woman who brought a girl to the Queen so that she could have her hair".

Bibl.: D., 460.

56

"*Marie Stuart.*" 1561. Black chalk with touches of yellow in the hair. 030×019. Bibliothèque Nationale, Cabinet des Estampes, Na. 22.

The Queen is shown in white mourning robes; she is a "white queen". The death of her husband, Francis II, had overwhelmed her, and she described herself as "the most wretched woman on earth", weighed down by "a grief too heavy for me to bear". She mourned for forty days in tomb-like solitude. Widowed on the 14th December, 1560, she left Paris on the 21st July, 1561.

Copies of this portrait, which immediately became famous, were sent to various Courts: Queen Elizabeth I received one soon after the death of Francis II; the King of Navarre had one at the Château of Pau (an Inventory of 1621, published by the A.A.F., Doc. 311, p. 60, mentions "a woman wearing white mourning robes"); while Ronsard, a fervent admirer of Mary Stuart, had one in his study, of which he tells us:

> "J'ai toutefois, pour chose plus rare . . .
> Dont mon étude et mes livres je pare,
> Votre semblant qui fait honneur au lieu
> Comme un portrait fait honneur à son Dieu."

(*Works*, 1567, vol. v, p. 144, ed. Marty-Laveaux).

Hist.: Formerly in coll. of the Abbey of Sainte-Geneviève.
Bibl.: Agnes Schikbusch, *Mary Stuart*, 1895, pp. 21, 35, 59, 164; Dimier, 465.

57

Elizabeth of Austria. 1571. Black and red chalk. 034×023. Bibliothèque Nationale, Cabinet des Estampes, Na. 22.

One of Clouet's last works (he died in 1572). This young Queen of France, who could only speak Spanish, was described by Brantôme as "a very fair princess with as fine a complexion as any lady at Court". P. A. Lemoisne, who speaks of "the atmosphere of quiet distilled from this sad gaze", is unwilling to give the drawing to Clouet, and upholds Moreau-Nélaton's attribution to Étienne du Moustier.

Bibl.: P. A. Lemoisne, *La Peinture au Musée du Louvre*, p. 56; D., 474.

AFTER FRANÇOIS CLOUET

58

Le malade imaginaire. About 1560–70. Black chalk. 016×017. Windsor, Royal Collection.

A sick man points to his stomach with one hand, and elbows aside his servant, who, hands on hips, make fun of him. The patient is obviously a writer of some sort, as is shown by the pen-holder and ink-horn hanging from his belt. Scene from a comedy as yet unidentified.

Drawing after François Clouet (died 1572) for an engraving by Le Blon of 1579 which is inscribed *Genet Inventor*.

Bibl.: J. Adhémar, "Deux Scènes de Comédie d'après Fr. Clouet", in *Graphische Kunste*, 1937, p. 136; A. E. Popham, "A Drawing by F. Clouet (?)", *ibid.*, 1939, p. 3; A. F. Blunt, *French Drawings at Windsor Castle*, 1945, pp. 16–17.

59

Self-portrait. About 1570. 265 × 190. Louvre, Cabinet des Dessins.

According to a tradition which, unfortunately, is not borne out by documents, this is said to be a portrait of Clouet, creator of so many of the portrait drawings reproduced in this book. Portraits of artists are extremely rare at this date, although there are two, one of Jean Clouet and one of the elderly Primaticcio, in existence.

Hist.: Inv. 25244.

60

Full-length portrait of Henry III. About 1571–72. Black chalk. 032 × 022. Bibliothèque Nationale, Cabinet des Estampes, Na. 21, fol. 92.

Inscribed "François de France, Duc d'Alençon" but identified by Dimier as a portrait of Henry III. Probably a study for one of the drawings which was sent to Queen Elizabeth I as an inducement to marry the King (see *Intro.*). The fact that the head and the body are drawn by two different hands is further proof of this, for Clouet sent two separate drawings, one of the head, and another of the body to show the King's commanding presence.

Bibl.: D., 473.

STUDIO OF NICCOLÒ DELL'ABBATE

61

Signing of a Treaty. About 1558. Pen and bistre wash with white highlights, squared. 028 × 037. Bibliothèque Nationale, Cabinet des Estampes.

On the strength of the inscriptions underneath the figures, Jal interpreted this drawing as Catherine de' Medici taking a pen from Étienne Du Moustier to sign a contract for two dwarfs, and dated it between 1559 and 1584. These dates do not coincide with those of Du Moustier, who was already thirty-eight in 1558 and not a boy in his twenties like the one in the drawing. Moreover, the small figures are too well proportioned to be dwarfs and are in fact a young Prince and Princess as a primitive painter might represent them. What we have here is the signing of a document by a widowed Queen and an ambassador; on stylistic evidence it dates from 1558–60. The Queen cannot be Catherine de' Medici, who was at that date older and heavier. It is possible, however, that this is a project for a picture intended for Mary of Lorraine, Queen of Scotland, and shows her receiving two ambassadors, possibly the Guise brothers, who have come to sign the marriage contract between Mary Stuart, then aged sixteen, and Francis II.

NICCOLÒ DELL'ABBATE
about 1512–71

62

A Prince on horseback. About 1560–70. Pen and bistre wash with white. 033 × 023. Chantilly, Musée Condé.

This is certainly not Charles IX, who had a very different face, but could be François, Duc de Guise (1519–63). Not only was he very like this man, but he was known to be the patron of Niccolò, to whom this Italianate work can be attributed with some probability.

Bibl.: Chantilly, 405; D., 1348 (without identification).

63

Rest on the Flight into Egypt. Pen-and-wash. 035 × 028. Vienna, Albertina.

A Bible subject treated so humanistically that all religious significance has disappeared. The high-water mark of Italian influence on the School of Fontainebleau.

Bibl.: A. Stix and A. Spitzmuller, *Albertina Cat.*, 1941, vol. VI, no. 38.

SCHOOL OF CORNEILLE DE LYON

64

Portrait of a woman. About 1580. Brush on toned paper, bluish background. 0,086×0,072. Paris, École des Beaux-Arts.

The woman's dress indicates that she is a rich and stylish *bourgeoise* of the late sixteenth century, but the technique is earlier and nearer in style to Corneille de Lyon. Possibly by his daughter.

Hist.: Masson Gift, no. 1049.

CORNEILLE DE LYON

about 1515–after 1574

65 (below)

Portrait of a man. About 1560–70. Red and black chalks. 0,230×0,182. Paris, École des Beaux-Arts.

This sad-faced bearded man differs from the usual Clouet or Court portrait. There is more feeling for the structure of the head, a more painterly approach which seems to confirm Masson's attribution to Corneille de Lyon. If the attribution is correct, this is his only known drawing.

Hist.: Masson Gift, no. 1048.

LAVINIA FONTANA

1552–1614

65 (above)

Portrait of a man wearing an aigrette. Black and red chalk. 0,071×0,046. Paris, École des Beaux-Arts.

The inscription "Lérinia de la Fontagne" at the bottom of the drawing refers not to the sitter but to the artist, Lavinia Fontana of Bologna (1552–1614). Her father Prospero Fontana (about 1512–87) was attracted to Paris at an unknown date by the example of Primaticcio, but became ill and did not stay long in France. It seems likely that he arrived about 1570, and that his daughter worked at Lyons with Corneille de Lyon who died four years later. More light might be thrown on this connection by a curious picture in the museum at Bologna: "Louise of Savoy, attended by four ladies-in-waiting, presents the future Francis I to his patron saint, Francis of Paola."

Hist.: Masson Gift, no. 1050.

ANTOINE CARON

about 1527–about 1599

66 (below)

The Artemisia Series. Pl. LXIII, *The Monument.* Pen over black chalk. 040×055. Bibliothèque Nationale, Cabinet des Estampes, Ad 105 rés.

One of the surviving thirty-nine drawings from a series commissioned by the rich *amateur* Nicolas Houel in honour of Catherine de' Medici who was as zealous a mother as Artemisia. The series, which is now incomplete, was drawn by Caron, probably after sketches by other artists; like Lerambert at a later date, he merely brought them into line. Many of the drawings were used as tapestry cartoons, but no tapestry is known to have been woven after this particular drawing. The monument in question is the Valois Rotonda at Saint-Denis, put up under the direction of Catherine de' Medici to house the remains of Henry II and his family.

66 (above)

"*On veit bien mille ouvriers . . .*" Pl. LX of the Artemisia Series. Pen over black chalk. 0,405 ×0,550. Bibliothèque Nationale, Cabinet des Estampes, Ad 105 rés.

There is a striking difference between the highly idealized, ancient architecture and the realism of the labourers. No tapestry is known to be woven after this design.

67 (below)

A procession carrying crowns. Pl. XV of the Artemisia Series. Pen over black chalk. 040×055. Bibliothèque Nationale, Cabinet des Estampes, Ad 105 rés.

In the background can be seen the Grotto of Meudon, which was completed in 1555. Guiffrey found a reference of 1792 to a tapestry woven after this scene, but none is now known to exist.

67 (above)

The capture of a fortress. Pl. LI of the Artemisia Series. Pen over black chalk. 0,405×0,550. Bibliothèque Nationale, Cabinet des Estampes, Ad 105 rés.

Tapestries were woven after this composition; one, mentioned in the 1792 Inventory of Crown possessions, was burnt in 1797. The fortress appears in the tapestries of the *Fêtes de Florence*, and in the drawing reproduced on plate 68.

68

Allegory. About 1580. Pen-and-ink. 039×023. Coll. G. Wildenstein.

Although inscribed "*Stephanus*" (Étienne Delaune), this drawing is probably by Caron. Jean Ehrmann has identified the Roman warrior as Naso, whose story is told by Appian (*Roman Wars*, trans. Seyssel, 1580, p. 341). Compare the fortress with that in the preceding drawing.

Hist.: Coll. Ch. Saunier.

69

The Triumph of War. About 1570. Pen-and-ink and black chalk. 032×048. Bibliothèque Nationale, Cabinet des Estampes, B 5 rés.

Drawing for a painting or tapestry. Possibly inspired by the Treaty of Saint-Germain, signed on the 8th August, 1570, which made peace between the Queen-Mother and the Protestants, proclaimed an amnesty and established the freedom of the reformed religion.

The need for this "shameful peace", as it was called by the Pope and Philip II, is implicit in this formidable spectacle of the triumph of Mars. The drawing agrees with Charles IX's maxim that conflicts could never be ended by mere force of arms.

70

Charles IX, wearing a laurel wreath, on horseback. 1560 (?). Black chalk. 030×020. Chantilly, Musée Condé.

Here one can accept the traditional attribution to Caron. The drawing appears to be a design for a bas-relief or an illusionist painting representing the young King crowned with laurel in the style of a Roman Emperor.

After the death of Henry II, probably as early as 1559, Catherine de' Medici had vacated the Royal Apartments at Fontainebleau for the new King and had another residence built in the *Jardin de Diane*. This must have been completed some time in 1560, since payments to Niccolò dell'Abbate for some landscapes were made in 1561. In Queen's Pavilion a room, called the *Cabinet des Empereurs*, was decorated with portraits of the twelve Roman Emperors (probably after Titian) and with one of the King. In the seventeenth century the French King represented was Henry IV, but in the sixteenth century it was Henry II. Ronsard, writing in 1560, described the picture as follows:

> "Quand, entre les Césars, j'aperçois ton image,
> Descouvrant tout le front de lauriers revêtu,
> Voyez, (ce dis-je alors) combien peut la vertu
> Qui fait d'un jeune Roy un César devant l'âge."

It seems likely that this drawing by Caron was intended to replace the portrait of Henry II by that of his successor, Charles IX, to whom Ronsard's lines apply equally well.

Bibl.: Chantilly, 396; D., 1309.

ANDROUET DU CERCEAU
about 1520–about 1585

71

Study for a chimney-piece. Pen-and-ink. 024×018. Louvre, Cabinet des Dessins.

This drawing for a high chimney-piece with a cartouche is evidence that Du Cerceau was one of the finest decorators of his period. Many of his drawings and drawings by his School have been preserved; Geymuller has catalogued them. The Cabinet des Estampes has one of his finest albums of drawings, the British Museum another.

Hist.: Inv. 33421.

72

The Château of Charleval. 1570–74. Pen-and-ink. 023×033. Bibliothèque Nationale, Cabinet des Estampes, B 5 rés.

Design for the main block of the Château of Charleval, Charles IX's favourite building project, which was situated in the forest near Les Andelys. He spent large sums of money on it during the last four years of his reign; the façade was to be over 390 feet long and the garden to cover about three-quarters of a mile. Two months after his death, work was abandoned. As Blunt has so justly remarked, Du Cerceau seems here to be more of a decorator than an architect—if he is in fact the architect of Charleval. Charles IX was partly responsible and many Italians were involved.

73 (above and below)

Palace of Les Tuileries. About 1564. Pen-and-ink. 011×043. London, British Museum.

Bird's-eye views of Philibert Delorme's project which was commissioned by the Queen in 1564 and never completed. When Delorme died in 1570, all that had been put up was the main entrance block and the two wings; Bullant and Le Vau modified this enormous scheme and did away with the inner courtyard.

Like Charleval, the Tuileries is a good example of one of those grandiose buildings that the later Valois dreamed up in the most troubled and uncertain years of their history. Threatened with difficulties both at home and abroad, with no money, no army, and a national debt of 50 millions, the Queen-Mother's reaction was to build this huge palace and go off on a royal progress with the Court and the young Charles IX. Ronsard too seemed confident:

> "Le Français semble au saule verdissant;
> Plus on le coupe et plus il est naissant,
> Et rejetonne en branches davantage."

Bibl.: W. H. Ward, *French Châteaux and Gardens in the XVIth Cent. . . .*, 1908; Y. Christ, *Le Louvre et les Tuileries*, p. 25.

FRENCH SCHOOL

74

Henry IV as a young man. About 1572. Coloured chalks. 034×024. Bibliothèque Nationale, Cabinet des Estampes, Na. 22.

This portrait by a painter of the French Court must date from July or August 1572, when the King's marriage took him to Paris. He was nineteen at the time and his mother wrote to him, "Try to train your hair upward, but not in the old-fashioned style." There was as yet no official painter at the Court of Navarre, which explains its dearth of portraits. In 1572, when Henry wanted a portrait of his future wife, Jeanne d'Albret wrote to him, "As for her painting, I shall send to Paris for it."

This charming portrait, which was identified by Bouchot, is given by Dimier to Du Moustier the uncle and dated about 1568. But both this and another from the same source have been attributed to Pierre Du Moustier.

Bibl.: H. Bouchot, *Les Portraits aux crayons*, p. 189; Maumené and d'Harcourt, *Iconographie des Rois de France*, vol. 1, pp. 223 and 228; D., 812.

SCHOOL OF FONTAINEBLEAU

75

Fruitfulness and Sterility. About 1570. Vienna, Albertina.

Attributed by Herr Hofmann to the School of Fontainebleau. It could be interpreted as an allusion to Elizabeth of Austria, who only gave her husband, Charles IX, one daughter, born in 1572, while in the following year his mistress, Marie Touchet, bore him a son, Charles de Valois, future commander of light cavalry. In any case, the artist seems to have a good knowledge of both Italian and Flemish Mannerists.

76

Bathing scene. About 1570. Black chalk with blue wash. 0,320×0,260. Louvre, Cabinet des Dessins. Probably German in inspiration (after engravings in the style of Durer), this drawing is interesting as an illustration of the various influences operating in the Fontainebleau School, especially in its attitude towards the female nude, the major artistic preoccupation of the time.

Hist.: Royal Coll. (*paraphe* of de Cotte); Inv. 8745 (formerly 7365).

77

Mythological subject. About 1570. Pen-and-wash. 032×033. Bibliothèque Nationale, Cabinet des Estampes, B 5 rés.

Landscape with a dryad pursued by a huntsman, possibly Aesacus and Hesperia, with Troy in the background:

"... quam Troius heros
Insequitur, celeremque metu celer urguet amore"
(Ovid, *Metamorphoses*, XI, 773–4).

This drawing, which is near in feeling to Cousin, belongs to a series of mythological subjects of which a number are preserved in the Cabinet des Estampes. Another passed through the L. Godefroy sale in 1927 (Cat., no. 21, 1927, no. 1309).

STYLE OF GERMAIN PILON

78

Drawing for a statue of "Aristoteles". About 1561. Black chalk. 0,340×0,270. Paris, École des Beaux-Arts.

Collections of drawings often contain studies, details of projects for tombs, which Colombier describes as being from the "agency" of Pilon. Decorative compositions, however, are rare. This particular drawing and three others, which included an *Allegory of Peace*, passed through the same sale (see J. Babelon, *Pilon*, no. 78).

This must be some sort of term, rather like those which supported the vine-arbour, also used as an aviary, in the *Jardin de la Reine* at Fontainebleau (1561).

The choice of the Greek philosopher is not unusual; it was probably pendant to a Plato, as was customary at the time. In 1539, Pietro Aretino sent two busts of Plato and Aristotle to the Cardinal of Lorraine; he in his turn gave them to the King, who was extremely interested.

Hist.: Coll. of V., sold the 13th February, 1908, Lot 181; Masson Coll. and Gift.

ÉTIENNE DUPÉRAC
about 1535–1604

79

Tivoli: the Temple of the Cascade. 1568. Pen-and-ink. 012×043. London, British Museum.

Drawn while Dupérac was living in Rome. He was a favourite of Cardinal Ippolito d'Este, who had just built his villa at Tivoli and who, according to Bertolotto, paid Dupérac 25 *écus "per fattura d'uno prospectiva del giardino di Tivoli, fatta in pittura sopra uno quadro sopra la tela"*. Later, in 1573, he was making an engraving of the villa and garden, dedicated to Catherine de' Medici, when the estate passed to Cardinal Luigi, Archbishop of Auch and Papal Legate in France, on the death of Ippolito. This landscape was therefore drawn from nature.

Bibl.: C. Dodgson in *O.M.D.*, June 1926; Egger, *Romische Veduten*, 1924, vol. II (with reference to a view of Rome).

JEAN COUSIN THE YOUNGER (?)

80

The miraculous draught of fishes. About 1570–80. Pen and bistre wash. 0,373×0,425. Paris, École des Beaux-Arts.

The story is written in contemporary handwriting at the bottom of the drawing. A design for a stained-glass window in the style of Jean Cousin the Elder, especially the engravings of the rue Montorgueil period.

Hist.: Masson Coll. and Gift, no. 874.

ÉTIENNE DU MOUSTIER
about 1520–1603

81

Self-portrait (?). About 1573. Coloured chalks. 036×027. Bibliothèque Nationale, Cabinet des Estampes, Na. rés., 23.t.I.

Close in style to a drawing of Du Moustier in Leningrad. The costume is characteristic of the reign of Henry III, and therefore cannot be earlier than 1573 when the artist was fifty years old. If this is so, it seems unlikely that this young man in Court dress is Du Moustier.

Hist.: Coll. Abbey of Sainte-Geneviève.
Bibl.: D., 805.

FRENCH SCHOOL
about 1570–80

82

Portrait of an unknown man. Black and red chalk. 026×021. Rheims, Museum.

This portrait bears two inscriptions at the top, one in chalk which says something like "Du Bele", and one in ink which says "pierre". This has been interpreted as meaning the father of Joachim du Bellay, but as the portrait dates from about 1570, when the Du Bellays, father and son, were both dead, this seems unlikely.

Actually this portrait, which Loriquet attributes to Daniel Dumoustier, is more probably by the Rheims painter Boba. It is also extremely close to a portrait of an unknown man by Corneille de Lyon in the Metropolitan Museum, New York. In both cases the man wears the tall Spanish-style hat which was fashionable in Germany and Flanders in the years 1570–80.

Hist.: Formerly in coll. of Rheims School of Drawing, founded in 1677; its mark centre right. Transferred to the Museum in 1795.
Bibl.: Loriquet, *Catalogue . . . du Musée de Reims,* 1881, p. 269, no. 37 of the drawings.

GEOFFROY DUMOUSTIER

83

Christ preaching. About 1543–47. Pen and bistre wash. 025×037. Paris, École des Beaux-Arts.

Design for stained-glass window. The Louvre possesses a *Mary Magdalen* in the same style.

Hist.: Coll. A.P.L.; Coll. Masson, exh. 1921, no. 191; Masson Gift, no. 3628.

FRENCH SCHOOL
1575

84

The Coronation of Henry III at Rheims, February 15, 1575. Black chalk and wash. 035×050. Coll. G. Wildenstein.

In Rheims Cathedral after his Coronation, the King receives Communion from the Cardinal de Guise, Archbishop of Metz, as the Archbishop of Rheims was not yet ordained.

Once crowned, Henry III showed great generosity towards the Cathedral, which in 1562 had donated 20,000 *livres* from its Treasury to "defend the Kingdom against the Huguenots". He in his turn presented the Cathedral with 500 *écus d'or* and a silver-gilt reliquary "the base of which is an agate with the eleven thousand virgins".

JEAN DECOURT
about 1530–about 1585

85

The Maréchale of Retz. 1577. Black chalk. 035×025. Bibliothèque Nationale, Cabinet des Estampes, Na. 22.

Jacques Lavaud's work on Desportes has enabled him to identify the painter of this cultivated woman, whose *salon* played an important part both in literature and religious affairs and had a great deal of influence on society. He attributes it to Jean Decourt, whose praises were sung by the *Maréchale's* friends; he was compared to Prometheus and Icarus for having dared to "pirate" such "sovereign beauty", such a "masterpiece" of nature. The portrait inspired several poems, including one offering from the provinces which read as follows:

> "Ce portrait excellent, cette belle effigie
> que j'aye vue à Paris m'a si fort transporté,
> qu'en plus loing de mon cour le sang s'est escarté,
> Rendant ma face blesme et mes esprits sans vie."

It will be seen from this how exaggerated were the literary tributes of the day to painters, who were habitually compared with Apelles.

FRENCH SCHOOL

86

"Louis de Beauveau de Tremblecour." Coloured chalks. 037 × 024. Bibliothèque Nationale, Cabinet des Estampes, Na. 21 rés., p. 116.

Executed with great care in order to satisfy the contemporary taste for an exact likeness and a more colourful drawing.

Hist.: From a Lot of drawings, attributed to *"Jannet"*, bought by Joly in 1825.

MARC DUVAL
1530–81

87

The three Coligny brothers. About 1579. Black chalk. 033 × 024. Bibliothèque Nationale, Cabinet des Estampes, Qb 407, p. 752.

Drawing for the engraving signed Marc Duval and dated 1579, whose popularity may be gauged by the many copies in existence.

The three brothers, sons of Gaspard de Coligny (1470–1522) were: Cardinal Odet de Chatillon (1517–71), François, Seigneur d'Andelot (1531–69) and Gaspard (1519–72). They had been dead for some years when Duval made this drawing after earlier portraits, for which he also may have been responsible. The drawing is a glorification of three great Huguenots, intended to be shown at the Conference of Nérac, where Catherine de' Medici tried to come to terms with the future Henry IV (December 1578–February 1579).

Hist.: Coll. Michel Hennin.
Bibl.: D., 766.

FRANÇOIS BUNEL
about 1550–about 1599

88

Henry IV. 1587. Black chalk with light touches of white. 0,140 × 0,110. Bibliothèque Nationale, Cabinet des Estampes, Hennin Collection.

Drawn at La Rochelle, where the King had "withdrawn into his shell" (Sully) before embarking on the attack which was to end with the Victory of Coutras. This portrait was rightly attributed to Bunel by Jacques de Laprade, who described it with some justice as "a lifeless drawing, with the accent on details such as the modelling of the lips, wrinkles, the height of the forehead and the bulge of the eyebrows" (*Revue des Arts*, 1953). In spite of this, the King was pleased with it and used it to popularize his cause in Italy and Germany. Annibale Carracci was ordered to engrave it and, to his astonishment, paid for the work, and was paid so well that he said "if all these works were worth that much he could have made a living without doing anything" (*Malvasia*, I, p. 85). The engraving, however, did not please Henry, and only a few prints were drawn from it. Another engraving was made by Gian Battista Mazza in 1589. In the meantime, the King had sent a copy of Bunel's drawing to the Queen of England. It is mentioned as being in her collection in 1624: "The Kynge Henri the IVth of France, done by Bonnel" (*G.B.A.*, 1868, vol. 1, p. 508), and from it Théodore de Bry made an engraving with slight differences in the King's appearance (hair, beard), only one copy survives and it is in the British Museum. The Queen was delighted with the portrait, as she told the French ambassador in 1590: "She led us into a secret room where she showed us your fine portrait, and she made such a fuss that it seemed to us as if she had some feeling for the original."

It has not yet been established whether the portrait of the King wearing a large hat (1590) is by Bunel, who by that date may have left for Tours.

Hist.: Coll. Hennin.

HENRI LERAMBERT
about 1550–about 1610

89

A Roman Triumph. About 1590. Ink over black chalk. 038 × 035. Bibliothèque Nationale, Cabinet des Estampes, B 5 rés.

Henri Lerambert, "Painter to the King" (Henry III) is mentioned by seventeenth-century historians as having made tapestry cartoons. In addition to a *Life of Christ* for the church of Saint-Merry, which Sauval saw on the looms in 1594, Félibien mentions an *Artemisia* and a *Coriolanus.*

Henri Lerambert is no doubt the son of Louis the Elder, the brother of Louis the Younger, the nephew of François, and the uncle of Louis III, Nicolas and Simon—the only painter in a family of sculptors, whose influence is seen in this frieze-like composition. This sculptural approach gives more body to the figures which derive ultimately from the Mannerism of Caron. It was, in fact, Lerambert who finished the latter's *Artemisia* series.

AMBROISE DUBOIS
1542/43–1614

90

The story of Theagenes: Chariclea before the King of Ethiopia. About 1598–60. Black chalk and bistre wash with some body-colour on toned paper. 0,328 ×0,451. Paris, École des Beaux-Arts.

One of the last episodes—it precedes the *Recognition of the Lovers*—of a Greek novel by Heliodorus, which was discovered in the sixteenth century and translated by Amyot. This tale of pirates, love and voyages had been quite popular under Henry II, but at the end of the century, after the Wars of Religion, it became fantastically successful. In 1629 (according to Adam), says Guez de Balzac, all the novels of the day "were mostly Heliodorus in disguise, or as the late Bishop of Aire used to say, children born of the union of Theagenes and Chariclea, and so like their parents that it was difficult to tell them apart".

This composition was not, whatever one may say, destined for the *Cabinet de Théagène* at Fontainebleau, although it might have been done for the Château of Saint-Germain.

Hist.: In the eighteenth century attributed to Parmigianino; Coll. Chennevières; Coll. Masson, exh. 1921, no. 59; Masson Gift, no. 905.

FRENCH SCHOOL
About 1590

91

Emmanuel Philippe of Lorraine, Duc de Mercœur. Black and red chalk. 035×025. Chantilly, Musée Condé.

Son of the Duc de Vaudemont and brother-in-law of Henry III (1558–1602). He started life as a member of the Catholic League, but went over to Henry IV and married his daughter to the King's natural son, César of Vendôme.

Hist.: Acquired with the Clouet drawings in the 1890's by the Duc d'Aumale.
Bibl.: M.N., 357.

BENJAMIN FOULON
about 1533–1600

92

"M. de Sully, Surintendant." About 1598. Coloured chalks. 033×023. Bibliothèque Nationale, Cabinet des Estampes, Na. 22.

Maximilien of Béthune, Duc de Sully (1559–1634), Henry IV's minister, is shown here at the peak of his career in 1598, when he was made *Surintendant des Finances.* He is known to have been extremely serious and to have disapproved of the King's insouciance. He said to him one day, "Good Heavens, Sire, . . . I have better things to think about than love or worry who is the most beautiful, and I'm sure the ladies do not think about my love or my beautiful nose any more than I do about theirs." He had little taste for the arts, and he shows it by having his portrait painted by the most mediocre of the Court painters.

Bibl.: D., 1159.

THE MASTER I.D.C.
working about 1590–1600

93

Gabrielle d'Estrées. Black and red chalk. 035×025. Bibliothèque Nationale, Cabinet des Estampes, Na. 22.

This charming woman had been Henry IV's mistress since 1593. He adored her and was so proud of her that he used to "show her off" to foreign ambassadors. She died in 1599 when she was about to marry him and become Queen of France.

This may be the preparatory drawing for a portrait which the King speaks of in a letter of 1598: "My dear love, I wrote to you at the feet of your portrait, which I adore only because it was done for you, not because it is like you. I am the best judge of this matter, for I have your image in all its perfection in my soul, in my heart and in my eyes."

She is seen wearing an enormous pearl ear-ring. She was very fond of jewels and the King gave her some wonderful pieces as, for example, a large "brooch in the shape of a sun consisting of one huge diamond" and a crystal chain made of fleurs-de-lis.

Bibl.: D., 1124.

LAGNEAU

94

Head of a man. Coloured chalks. 040 × 027. Chantilly, Musée Condé.

Lagneau, of whom G. Parisot is making a study, is still a very shadowy figure. This drawing, in which he has merely emphasized the wrinkles and warts of his model, does not show him at his satirical best.

His work coincides with the aftermath of the Wars of Religion, when a satirical and comic spirit was abroad. He should be compared with the poet Sigogne (died 1611), who was the author of a poem on a courtier's nose and of an "*Anatomie du Manteau de Court*". Antoine Adam would doubtless compare him with the "smutty poets" of Queen Marguerite's circle. The drawn and engraved caricatures which began to be frequent at this period should not be overlooked.

MARTIN FRÉMINET
1567–1619

95

The Resurrection. About 1598. Pen and bistre wash with some body-colour on toned paper. 0,490 × 0,362. Paris, École des Beaux-Arts.

Hist.: Masson Gift, no. 927.

JEAN BOUCHER
1563–1633

96

Pan and Syrinx. 1600. Red chalk. 017 × 021. Paris, École des Beaux-Arts.

Hist.: Masson Coll. and Gift, no. 800; Masson Gift Exh., 1936, no. 7.

ABBREVIATIONS

B.A.F.: *Bulletin de la Société de l'Histoire de l'Art français*

B.N.: Bibliothèque Nationale, Paris

Burl. Mag.: *Burlington Magazine*

Cat. ms.: Manuscript catalogue of the drawings in the Louvre

Chantilly: Manuscript inventory of the drawings in the Musée Condé, Chantilly

D.: Louis Dimier: *Histoire de la peinture de portrait en France, au XVIe siècle*

Dimier: Louis Dimier: *Le Primatice.* 1900

G.B.A.: *Gazette des Beaux-Arts.*

G. Ring: Grete Ring: *A Century of French Painting.* London. 1949

M.N.: Moreau-Nélaton: *Les Clouet et leurs émules.* 1924. 3 volumes

O.M.D.: *Old Master Drawings.* Review

LIST OF ARTISTS